JEWISH ENCOUNTERS

Jewish Encounters is a collaboration between Schocken and Nextbook, a project devoted to the promotion of Jewish literature, culture, and ideas.

>nextbook

# PUBLISHED

# FORTHCOMING

---

*Abraham*

## ALSO BY ALAN DERSHOWITZ

# ALAN M. DERSHOWITZ

# ABRAHAM

The World's First (But Certainly Not Last)
Jewish Lawyer

NEXTBOOK · SCHOCKEN · NEW YORK

Schocken Books and colophon are registered trademarks of
Penguin Random House LLC.

Library of Congress Cataloging-in-Publication Data
Dershowitz, Alan M., author.
Abraham : the world's first (but certainly not last) Jewish lawyer / Alan M.
Dershowitz.
    pages cm.
    Includes bibliographical references and index.
    ISBN 978-0-8052-4293-5 (hardcover : alk. paper). ISBN 978-0-8052-4331-4
(eBook).
    1. Jews—Legal status, laws, etc.—History.  2. Jewish lawyers—
History.  3. Abraham (Biblical patriarch).  I. Title.
    K3242.D47 2015      340.092'3924—dc23      2015004649

www.schocken.com

Jacket image: *Abraham* by Joseph Schonmon
Photo: Sedmak/iStock/Getty Images
Jacket design by Oliver Munday

Printed in the United States of America
First Edition

2  4  6  8  9  7  5  3

*To Irwin Cotler—a modern-day Abraham—
and to all courageous lawyers, Jewish and non-Jewish,
who boldly confront injustice
and who aggressively demand a single standard of justice*

# CONTENTS

# INTRODUCTION

## The Jewish Lawyer

braham, the world's first Jew, was also the world's first lawyer, arguing with God on behalf of the doomed sinners of Sodom. He was
thus the first in a long line of Jewish lawyers. Joseph soon followed, serving as a counsel to the powerful, as many Jewish lawyers have done since.[1]
Then came Moses, who was not only a lawgiver but also an advocate on
behalf of Jews who had rejected him, his laws, and his God.[2] Daniel, who
in the Apocrypha serves as a defense lawyer to Susanna, perfected a tech-
nique of cross-examination that is still effectively used today.[3] And Deborah the judge dispensed justice under a palm tree.[4] But Abraham was the
first, and this book is about him and his progeny: the numerous Jewish
lawyers who—for better or worse, but in my view mostly better—have
changed the world by challenging the status quo, defending the unpopular, contributing to the rule of law, and following the biblical command
to pursue justice.

The story of Abraham is the account of a complex man whose actions
and inactions reflect the very different archetypes of the Jewish lawyer
over time and place. No one knows, of course, whether the Abraham we
know from the Bible ever really existed or whether he is a mythical or
composite figure. Nor would it ever be possible to challenge the biblical account of Abraham historically,[5] because—unlike the New Testament and Qur'anic accounts of Jesus and Muhammad—it takes place well
before modern recorded history.[6] In any event, it really doesn't matter,
unless one is a biblical literalist. Neither does it matter, for purposes of
this book, whether the Bible was written by the singular hand of God or

by multiple human authors. What matters is that the biblical Abraham has been and remains one of the most influential characters in history, whether or not he was an actual historical figure. His story stands as a cornerstone of three great religions and has influenced, and continues to influence, billions of people. Abraham matters—to Jews, to Christians, to Muslims, and to all who study the Bible or the Qur'an. And so this book will treat the biblical narrative as gospel (or, as lawyers might put it, the transcript of testimony).

The biblical account of the patriarch of the three great "Abrahamic" religions—Judaism, Christianity, and Islam[7]—comprises several overlapping subplots, some of which are in the text itself, while others are based on midrashic[8] and other authoritative commentaries. Each of these subplots reflects a different characteristic of lawyers in general and Jewish lawyers in particular.

The biblical Abraham, like so many Jewish lawyers throughout history, was an immigrant. He left his "parents' home" and, along with his nephew Lot, made aliya to a promised Jewish homeland, thus also becoming the world's first Zionist. Like other immigrants, he changed his name—from Abram to Abraham. He also changed his religion, shattering his father's idols (according to a midrashic addendum to the text of the Bible) and making a covenant with a new God. By destroying these icons, Abraham became the first "iconoclast," a term applied to many Jewish lawyers throughout history who have shattered idols—both religious and secular—ever since Abraham showed the way. Why have so many Jewish lawyers broken with tradition and challenged established doctrines? Perhaps understanding Abraham will give us a clue.

Before long, Abraham challenged the authority, indeed the morality, of his new God and accused Him—as so many Jewish lawyers have accused authority—of applying a double standard of justice and acting hypocritically: "How dare You, the Judge of all the world, not Yourself do justice!"[9] In speaking to God in this manner, he demonstrated the quintessential characteristic that has come to be associated with the Jewish lawyer: chutzpah. Indeed, the word "chutzpah" is first used to describe

Abraham's challenge to God. In the Aramaic words of the Talmud, Abraham demonstrated "chutzpah k'lapey shmaya"—chutzpah even in his dealings with the heavenly.[10]

In later years, Jews have put God on trial for breaking His covenant with the Jewish people and for allowing crusades, inquisitions, pogroms, and the Holocaust. Although God has not fared well in these moot court proceedings, those who put Him on trial generally continued to believe in Him, as Abraham did. Others, however, lost faith in a God who could stand idly by such evil. Why did some choose Abraham's path while others chose its opposite? Understanding Abraham may offer an explanation.

Because he argued with God on behalf of the sinners of Sodom, one would surely have expected Abraham to argue with those who would order the deaths of innocent children. But Abraham twice remained silent in the face of immoral demands that he engage in acts that risked the lives of his two innocent sons. The first demand came from his wife, Sarah, to cast out his son Ishmael—born to his Egyptian handmaid Hagar—into the wilderness, where the child faced likely death. Although the demand was displeasing to Abraham, he followed it because God told him to do whatever Sarah asked (thus invoking the stereotype of the "henpecked" Jewish husband; there is an old joke about the Jewish kid who tells his mother that he was cast in the role of the Jewish husband in a school play, to which the disappointed mother replies, "I was hoping you would get a speaking part"). God also assured him that the progeny of both Isaac and Ishmael would become great nations, and God eventually intervened to save Ishmael and Hagar.

The second immoral demand came directly from God: that Abraham offer to sacrifice his (and Sarah's) beloved and totally innocent son, Isaac. Abraham again remained silent in the face of God's outrageous command—a command that well deserved the rebuke Abraham had previously directed at God if He were to sweep away the innocent along with the guilty.

Suddenly Abraham, the radical iconoclast and chutzpahnik lawyer, appears to transform himself from one willing to challenge his God into a compliant fundamentalist who elevates dogma over reason, faith over morality. He willingly follows orders that will result in the death of the innocent, thereby becoming a Jew who is willing to sacrifice other Jews—indeed, his own flesh and blood—in order to remain in the good graces of an authority figure whom he fears. Abraham succeeded in that regard, earning for his refusal to speak morality to authority the praise of God's angel: "For now I know that you fear God, since you have not withheld your son, your favored one, from Me." Tragically, this cowering before power has characterized far too many Jewish lawyers throughout history.

This dichotomy between standing up for the rights of others—in this case the sinners of Sodom—while refusing to help fellow Jews has also been characteristic of some Jewish lawyers who have rejected the wise teaching of Hillel to balance the support for others with advocacy for one's own people.[11] The question is why. Perhaps by exploring the answers suggested by commentators on the Abraham story, we can begin to understand the broader paradox with regard to Jewish lawyers and leaders.

As we will see in the chapters to come, Abraham's actions reflect other characteristics, both good and bad, long associated with the Jewish lawyer: he is clever, somewhat conniving, a good negotiator, a sharp real estate lawyer, a man who knows how to manipulate the law and the facts and how to use irony to make a point. He is also a lawyer who knows when to stop arguing—when to settle a case in order to secure a partial victory. We will see how these characteristics have become stereotypes—some positive, some negative—employed with respect to Jewish lawyers and Jews in general. When it comes to Jews, even the most positive of traits have been turned into negatives.[12] The question again is why. Exploring in depth the complexity of the world's first Jewish lawyer may provide some clues.

If Christianity is a religion of grace and Islam is a religion of submission, then Judaism is a religion of law. To be an observant Jew, one must obey the rules—the 613 biblical mitzvoth plus the thousands of rabbinic rules designed to build "fences" around the core prohibitions.[13]

Jewish law is highly technical, with about half of it constituting detailed prohibitions, while the other half concocts equally detailed ways around the prohibitions—something like the Internal Revenue Code. No wonder so many Jews become lawyers. Is it in their DNA? In their religious training? In their experience? Or in a combination of these?

It is certainly in their history of being the victims of persecution. The Jewish people—individual Jews and now the nation-state of the Jewish people—always seem to be on trial for something. One prominent commentator on the Bible titled his book *The Last Trial*,[14] but the "trial" of Abraham was only the first of countless trials in which the Jewish people have been placed in the dock of justice or injustice.

The Jewish people have been accused of killing Jesus. The Jews of Spain and other countries were put on trial during the Inquisition. In the Middle Ages, there were the infamous disputations, which were a form of trial. Then there were the blood libels, which were centered in Europe but extended to other parts of the world. In France, there was the trial of Alfred Dreyfus, and in America, of Leo Frank, in which individual Jews were in the dock, but the Jewish people were also on trial. During the Holocaust, European Jewry was executed without even being put on trial, while many in the world tried and condemned the victims for going "like sheep" to their deaths. During the 1930s, 1940s, and 1950s, Stalin placed many Jewish intellectuals and leaders on trial, allegedly for being cosmopolitans and nationalists but really for being Jews. In the 1960s, Hannah Arendt used the trial of Adolf Eichmann as a vehicle for placing Jewish leaders in the dock for their actions and inactions during the Holocaust[15] (without mentioning her own love affair and rehabilitation of a leading Nazi intellectual, Martin Heidegger).[16] During the 1970s and 1980s, many Soviet Jews were placed on trial for being refuseniks and dissidents.[17]

Most recently, the nation-state of the Jewish people seems always to be on trial, both in the court of public opinion and before international tribunals and the United Nations.[18]

Why have Jews been singled out—chosen?—for persecution, for trials, and for the application of the double standard? Is it because they proclaim their chosenness? Is it because they have been so successful in the most visible of professions? Is it because they have endured so many trials? Is it because for so many centuries they were incapable of fighting back? Is it now because—finally—they have a powerful nation-state that *is* capable of defending itself and fighting back? Is it simply because we are Jews?

Whatever the reasons, the reality is that we Jews—more than others—need advocates such as Abraham to defend us against these and other false charges. Fortunately, we have always had our defenders, generally Jewish lawyers, sometimes not. Will we continue to? Or will Jewish lawyers, like other secular Jews, begin to disappear through assimilation?

Whether because of our religious training, our history, or other factors, many Jews—it turns out—make darn good lawyers. In every nation in which Jews have had a significant presence, they have been among the leaders of the bar (as well as of other vocations, ranging from medicine to comedy). That is certainly true today in the United States, Great Britain, France, Australia, South Africa, and other Western nations. But it was also true in North Africa during the first half of the twentieth century, in Weimar Germany, in czarist Russia, and in many parts of central Europe.

We've had a lot of practice, as a people, in defending ourselves, but also in defending others. Jews have been at the forefront not only of the commercial bar but also of the human rights, civil rights, and civil liberties movements.[19] We have also been leaders in the continuing effort to promote the rule of law as a universal principle of justice. It all began with the world's first lawyer, Abraham, whose life, as narrated in the Bible, the Qur'an, and the commentaries, I now recount.

# PART I

---

## The Biblical Narrative:
## The Lawyer Abraham

# 1

## God Meets Abram—and So Do We

We are introduced to Abraham, born Abram, through his genealogy and place of origin.[1] His lineage is traced to Noah's first son, Shem. Abram's father was Terah, who took him, his wife, and his brother's son Lot from Ur in the direction of Canaan before they settled in Haran, from where God directed Abram to continue on his journey to the promised land.

### The Prequel

When God first calls Abram, he is an old man, married to Sarai, an old woman who is barren. We are told little else about the unlikely man who is chosen by God to be the patriarch of great nations and religions—unlikely because of his apparent inability to become a "patriarch" in light of his and his wife's procreationally challenging advanced age.

The rabbis understandably ask, "Why Abram?" The text provides no answer. Even if God could miraculously cause Sarai to bear Abram's child, there is nothing we are told about Abram that would seem to qualify him for his important new role. Unlike with Noah, who was "righteous among his generation," Abram has no apparent merit that would warrant his selection by God from among the others of his generation. The rabbis therefore must imagine a reason: namely, that even as a young man, Abram must have been ready to accept the singular Jewish God in place of his father's idols. They then construct an engaging narrative—a prequel that is hardly hinted at in the text[2]—that also shows the young Abram's lawyerly mind, ready to use an advocate's gambit to justify his bold act of civil and parental disobedience.[3]

We also see Abram placed on trial for his religious deviation from the accepted norm—a tradition that would continue down through the generations of Abram's descendants, who have repeatedly stood in the dock of history.

According to the midrashic account, Abram's father, like the fathers of so many modern lawyers, was engaged in an old-fashioned business that was embarrassing to his son: he manufactured and sold clay idols. (When I was growing up in Brooklyn, the father of one of my close friends manufactured Christian religious figures. He called them "goyisher tchotchkes" and defended his job, proclaiming, "It's a living!") Like Cordelia in Shakespeare's greatest play, *King Lear*, Abram elevates his conception of truth over his obligation to his father, thereby breaking not only his father's idols but also the Fifth Commandment,[4] to honor and obey one's father and mother.[5]

Terah was understandably upset at the loss of his inventory and asked his son, "Who smashed the idols?" The clever young man laid a trap for his unwary father: "The largest idol must have done it" (thereby breaking the spirit of yet another commandment: not to bear false witness). To which his father responded, "Clay idols have no power over other idols," thus creating an "aha moment" for the aspiring young lawyer. "Then why do you worship such powerless objects?" he asked rhetorically, if disrespectfully, thus winning the argument but at the cost of humiliating his father—another phenomenon that often characterizes generational differences between Jewish lawyers and their less educated parents.[6] According to the Midrash, Abram's father, unable to refute his son's logic, turns him over to King Nimrod, who places him "on trial" and sentences the young blasphemer to "the flames," from which he emerges unscathed.[7] It is ironic that Terah's decision to sacrifice young Abram to Nimrod—thereby placing his loyalty to his own faith (idolatry) above his love for his child—set a tragic example for Abraham, who would place loyalty to his God above his love for his own sons Ishmael and Isaac.[8]

The scene of the "wise guy" son one-upping his father with a verbal trap is reminiscent of latter-day Jewish humor, ranging from Sholem Aleichem to the Marx Brothers to Seinfeld. Samson Raphael Hirsch, a nineteenth-century German rabbi, commented on another sarcastic biblical put-down reminiscent of Abram's when Pharaoh's army was closing in on the Israelites and one Israelite sarcastically quipped, "Was it because there were no graves in Egypt that you brought us to the desert to die?"[9] Hirsch observed, "This sharp irony even in a moment of deepest anxiety and despair marks the sense of wit that is a characteristic trait of the clearheaded Tribe of Jacob."[10]

Abram, who would soon be arguing with a far more brilliant interlocutor, thus experienced his first verbal victory, whether by deception or sarcasm. It would not be his last.

By smashing his father's idols, Abram demonstrated his merit to God in several ways: he was open to new religious experiences, rather than accepting the established tradition; he had a mind-set ready to accept a living, intervening, and interactive God; he was prepared to speak truth to power; and he was intelligent and capable of defending himself against accusations, whether true or false—and winning.

God's chosen messenger—and his successors—would have to smash many idols, defend against many accusations, and escape many flames if God's prophecy for the Jewish people was to be fulfilled. Abram was God's kind of guy. God picked wisely and well, even if Abram would not always agree with Him. God didn't want a lackey. He wanted a partner, and in Abram, He found one.

## Abraham Enters into a Series of Contracts—Covenants—with God

Contract is the beginning of democracy. In a transforming thesis known as "From Status to Contract," the nineteenth-century legal philosopher Henry Sumner Maine famously argued that ancient societies, which were based on hierarchical and relatively permanent differences in status, moved toward modern democracy by relying more on agreements that required the mutual consent of the contracting parties.[11] The relationship between God and the Jewish people, even in ancient times, has always been viewed through the metaphor of contract or covenant. God asks something of His people and offers something in return. God's relationship with Abraham was, from the very beginning, contractual. God asks of Abram that he leave the place where he had settled with his family. In exchange, God promises to lead him to a new land, where He will make of him a great nation, which will become a litmus test of morality, because God promises to "bless those who bless you, and curse him that curses you." The modern State of Israel—the nation of the Jewish people—has certainly proved to be an important litmus test of the morality of nations, groups, and individuals.[12]

God also promises the entire land—its length and breadth—to Abram and his descendants. This promise has, of course, engendered great controversy over the millennia since it was made. Others too have claimed the imprimatur of a divine land grant,[13] but the text of the Bible, for those who believe it represents God's word, seems unambiguous: If God created the world and assigned its component parts to different nations, then what is now the land of Israel (and more) was assigned by God to the Jewish people.[14] Moreover, He did so by contract, because Abram gave up much in reliance on God's promise, leaving his birthplace and enduring many challenges and much travail on his mandated journey to the promised—or contracted—land. There was thus "consideration," "reliance," and a "meeting of the minds"—the basic and universal elements of a binding contract.[15] There was even the symbolism that was deemed essential in the ancient world: a smoking oven and a flaming torch to light the darkened sky.[16] As one Christian commentator put it, "As the law contains rewards and punishments, it was given in the midst of fire to indicate that it brings burning to some and illumination to others. . . . [It] burns those who abandon it, and enlightens those who observe it."[17] Eventually, God even got Abram to change his name to Abraham—adding the letter *hey* (the equivalent of *h*) to signify God's name. Sarai did the same, changing her name to Sarah. This God-imposed name change is reminiscent of the old joke about Finkelstein, the poor tailor, who prayed that God give a lift to his dwindling business. God whispered in his ear, "Make wide lapels." Finkelstein took the advice, and his business saw a huge surge. Eventually, the trend went out of fashion, and Finkelstein beseeched God again. This time God whispered, "Make narrow ties." Soon this became the hottest trend. The next week in synagogue, Finkelstein the tailor thanked God and announced that he would rename his store "Finkelstein and God" to honor Him. God whispered in his ear, "No, we need a catchier name. Call it Lord and Taylor."

## God Keeps His Side of the Deal, with the Help of Abraham's Connivance

Before Abraham could become the patriarch of a great people who would populate the land of Israel, several barriers had to be overcome. The commentators posit ten tests he had to pass. The first required him to deal with both natural and human challenges. The natural challenge was a severe famine in the promised land, necessitating travel to a more fertile location, Egypt. (Did Abram violate God's command by leaving Canaan for Egypt, as some commentators have suggested?[18] Perhaps, as evidenced by God's subsequent command to Isaac during another famine: "Do not go down to Egypt." In other words, don't make the same mistake your dad did—look at the trouble it got him into!) The Egyptians were known to kill the husbands of desirable women so as to take the women for themselves. That gave rise to the human challenge. Abram had to figure out a way to make it to the lifesaving nutriment of Egypt without losing his life, and his wife, to Egyptian predators. If he did not overcome these barriers, God's prophecy could not be fulfilled, because the barren Sarai had not yet borne him any progeny—the next barrier he would have to overcome, if he made it through Egypt.

The wily Abram came up with a plan. Like other lawyers throughout history, he prepared his witness, coaching his wife to say she was his sister. Abram obviously understood something that makes little sense to the contemporary ear: that the "brother" of a beautiful woman would be treated better by predatory men than her husband would be.[19] This was apparently because the taboo against having sex with a married woman was stronger in some parts of the ancient world than the taboo against killing her husband. Thus a predatory king would have the husband killed, thereby making the object of his desire a sexually "available widow."[20] Whatever the cultural reason, the ploy worked—at least for Abram.[21] Pharaoh's subjects took Sarai to Pharaoh's home,[22] where she presumably became part of his harem, though this is not explicitly stated in the text. What is stated is that as a result of this transaction, Abram was given sheep, oxen, camels, and slaves, both male and female. This commodification of Sarai is not further mentioned, and it is left to the reader's imagination what Pharaoh got from Sarai in exchange for these valuable goods being given to her husband/brother (procurer?). We can gather some further clue from what then befell Pharaoh: "The Lord afflicted Pharaoh and his household with mighty plagues on account of [what he had done to] Sarai, the wife of Abram."

At that point, Pharaoh figured out that Sarai must be Abram's wife—not his sister—and that he had been tricked into having a relationship of which a powerful and punishing God disapproved. Because this God was the God of Abram and Sarai, Pharaoh felt that the safest course was to be rid of the troublesome couple, so he sent them away, not wanting once again to incur the wrath of their vengeful God. Abram thus used his lawyerly wiles against a powerful king to save his own life and to keep God's contractual prophecy alive.[23]

Nor would this be the last time Abram played the sister card. Later in the narrative, when Abraham and Sarah—whose names had now been changed—again wandered, they entered the land ruled by Abimelech. Again Abraham described his wife as his sister, and again the king took her into his home.[24] But this time the text is clear: Abimelech had "not approached" Sarah. (No such assurance is given with regard to Pharaoh.)

God warns Abimelech in a dream that he will die because the woman he has taken is married. Abimelech offers two legal defenses: to the charge of adultery, he correctly points out that he has not yet committed the completed crime, because he never touched her; as to the inchoate crime of "attempted adultery"—or, as the Christian Bible would later put it, "adultery in the heart"—he pleads "mistake of fact," claiming that his "heart was blameless" because he honestly believed Sarah was Abraham's sister and not his wife.

Echoing what was to be Abraham's argument with God over the sinners of Sodom, Abimelech rhetorically asks, "Lord, will You slay people even though innocent?"

God accepts Abimelech's legal defenses and agrees to spare him if he restores Sarah to Abraham and frees them both, which he agrees to do, but not before confronting Abraham with his own crime—getting Abimelech in trouble with God by lying to him about Sarah's status: "What have you done to us? What wrong have I done you that you should bring so great a guilt upon me and my kingdom?[25] You have done to me things that ought not to be done. What, then, was your purpose in doing this thing?" Abraham responds to this serious accusation—a variation on the bearing of false witness or entrapment—by first claiming the defense of "necessity": "I thought . . . they will kill me because of my wife." (The defense of necessity justifies some lesser crimes to prevent greater harms, such as death.) He then compounds his initial lie with what appears to be a second lie: "She is in truth my sister, my father's daughter though not my mother's; and she became my wife."

The commentators have considerable difficulty with this defense, because it raises the possibility that by marrying Sarah, Abraham might have been committing incest,[26] at least under Jewish law as it was later codified in subsequent books of the Bible.[27] If this was to be true, the legitimacy of the entire progeny of Abraham and Sarah would be called into question, and the Arab/Muslim claim that God's promise was fulfilled through Abraham's son Ishmael, rather than through Isaac, who under this theory would be the product of incest, would be strengthened.

It is not surprising therefore that the "lying sister theory" (or at least a *misleading* sister theory) is generally preferred over the "truthful incest theory"—though some have claimed that marriage to the daughter of a father, but not mother, was not incest under ancient (pre-Sinai) rules.[28] In either event, these two "sister" stories—taken together, though they are separated in the narrative by considerable time and important events— present a calculating and shrewd Abraham prepared to bend the rules and stretch the truth to save his life. He is also prepared to place at risk his wife's sexual purity in the interests of a higher calling—namely, to help God's prophecy become a reality.

Abraham was, of course, aware of God's prophecy. He also knew that it could not be achieved unless he remained alive and capable of procreating with Sarah (he had already procreated with Hagar by the time of the second sister gambit, but he knew that Ishmael would not be the progenitor of the Jewish people).

This dilemma raises the theological quandary of "whether the promises made by God absolve human beings from taking measures that seem necessary to bring about the promises."[29] To translate this biblical dilemma into contemporary language, Professor Jon Levenson retells a version of my mother's favorite joke about the old Jew who prays to God to win the lottery once in his lifetime. On his deathbed, he rails against God: "All my life I prayed for one thing—to win the lottery—and you wouldn't even give me that." God replies, "You could have helped me by buying a ticket."[30]

Whether or not Abraham "bought a ticket" by playing the sister card, the future patriarch was certainly prepared to engage in conduct that reflects a selfish "ends justifies the means" philosophy, which seems more suited to a crafty lawyer than to a prophet of God. This too is part of the legacy of Abraham as the world's first Jewish lawyer.

Eventually, Abraham prays on Abimelech's behalf, and God heals Abimelech, his wife, and their maids. A midrash points out that this is the first example in the Bible of someone's praying on behalf of another.[31] Abraham, the first Jewish advocate, is prepared to use all the tools of persuasion, from trickery to prayer. As we shall see, he would soon employ an even bolder form of advocacy.

## The Wars of the Kings and the Rescue of Lot

An oft-neglected aspect of the Abraham narrative involves his role as rescuer of his kinfolk during a war between the kings. The Bible describes a series of battles among the kings of the various nations that inhabited the lands near where Abraham—then still Abram—had settled. The relevance of these conflicts seems unclear at the beginning of the story, but then the narrator informs us that the invaders "took Lot, the son of Abram's brother." When Abram learns of this, he springs into action, mustering his small army of retainers to rescue his nephew. Abram's army, numbering 318, defeats those who had taken Lot and his family and rescues them, gaining the praise and respect of other kings and allowing him to perform what would become one of the cardinal mitzvoth—praiseworthy deeds—of the Jewish tradition: *pidyon shvuim*, the rescue of captives.

Here too Abraham paved a road that many Jewish lawyers, and eventually the modern Jewish state, would follow: the rescue of fellow Jews, and others, from captivity and danger, whether it be from pogroms, the Holocaust, the terrorism of Entebbe, the Soviet Gulag, or capture by Hamas or Hezbollah. The tradition of leaving no soldier or citizen in the hands of enemies has characterized the Jewish state and finds its inspiration in the actions of Abraham.

# 2

---

## God Tests Abraham and Abraham
## Passes—at Least the First Test

In light of Abraham's willingness to deceive others in the interest of saving himself (as he did in the first sister story and as he would later do in the second) and to use military force in the interest of rescuing his nephew, God must have wondered[1] whether Abraham was the right choice to bring God's message of justice to the world. God devised a test, therefore, to determine whether Abraham could be counted on to teach the world how to strike a proper balance between protecting one's own interests and defending the rights of others—a balance that would later be articulated by Hillel in his famous dictum "If I am not for myself, who will be for me? But if I am for myself alone, what am I?"[2]

God therefore decides to gauge Abraham's reaction to a punishment He is planning to inflict on the sinners of Sodom. God decides not to conceal from Abraham what He is considering doing to the city if, after conducting a personal investigation, He determines that the "outcry" He is hearing about its people's outrageous conduct is true. Even God doesn't accept hearsay evidence of a serious crime. According to Rashi,[3] God's decision to "descend and see" is meant as a lesson to human judges that they must insist on seeing evidence themselves.[4] God then tells us why He is revealing His plans to Abraham:

> I have singled him out, that he may instruct his children and his posterity to keep the way of the Lord by doing what is just and

right, in order that the Lord may bring about for Abraham what He has promised him.

In other words, this test was designed to provide the patriarch of a great nation that will be a light unto other nations an object lesson in justice so that he can then "instruct his children and his posterity" both "to keep the way of the Lord" and to do "what is just."[5] It was a challenging test because God deliberately constructed a scenario in which there was a direct conflict between keeping the way of the Lord and doing justice. Abraham could not do both. He had to choose between accepting God's expressed view of "what is just" and his own view that what God was preparing to do was not just. In constructing this test, God was doing what law professors and rabbinic scholars have done throughout history: devising challenges, generally in the form of hypothetical scenarios, that have no perfect solutions and that require a tragic choice between "the lesser of two evils."

God, the great teacher, understood that the best way to instill into a person a deep sense of justice is to expose him or her to the real prospect of injustice. One's sense of justice derives from exposure to injustice, just as one's sense of right (and rights) comes from exposures to wrongs.[6] Moreover, being forced to argue against a powerful authority figure gives the person a real stake—both intellectual and emotional—in the merits of his argument.[7]

Abraham—unlike Noah, who saved his own family without questioning God's decision to sweep away the remainder of humanity, regardless of individual guilt—passes the test with flying colors and in the process establishes himself as the patriarch of the legal profession: a defense lawyer for the damned who is willing to risk everything, even the wrath of God, in defense of his clients. When God tells him of His plan, Abraham "comes forward"[8] and issues a direct rebuke[9] to his newfound God and contracting partner:

Will You sweep away the innocent along with the guilty? What if there should be fifty innocent within the city; will You then wipe out the place and not forgive it for the sake of the innocent fifty who are in it? Far be it from You to do such a thing, to bring death upon the innocent as well as the guilty so that innocent and guilty fare alike. Far be it from You! Shall not the Judge of all the earth deal justly?[10]

Wow! Is there any other religious tradition[11] in which a human being speaks so disrespectfully to his God—and to His face?[12] (The authors of the midrash might well have derived the Abram who confronts his father so disrespectfully from this later Abraham who challenges God with a mixture of disrespect and respect.) Indeed, the standard translations—which employ the euphemistic words "far be it from You" to translate the far more powerful words "chalila l'cha"—do not do justice (pun intended) to the original Hebrew.

The root of the word *chalila*, which Abraham twice directs at God in a single rebuke, is "to profane." Its most common usage is to condemn a human being (generally a Jew) for profaning (or disgracing) God Himself by his ungodly actions. A Jew who does this commits a "chilul Hashem," which is about the worst rebuke one Jew can direct at another.[13] Yet Abraham directs his accusation of profanation at God Himself.[14] To be sure, it is a *conditional* rebuke: If you *were* to sweep away the innocent along with the guilty, You *would then* be guilty of profaning justice. But recall that this God had *already* once before done just that: after regretting the creation of human beings, He swept away the entire population of the world—including babies and children, those physically and mentally incapable of sinning—during the Flood, saving only the family of one relatively righteous man.

Was Abraham rebuking God not only *conditionally*, on the basis of what He *might* do in the future, but also *unconditionally*, for what He had *already* done in the past? Perhaps, but we can never know, because Abraham did what good lawyers often do: he covered his rear end by expressly conditioning his rebuke on future conduct while leaving open the possibility that he intended to condemn past conduct as well. Pretty clever! Abraham also surrounded his aggressive language with conciliatory words, such as "Now pray, I have ventured to speak to my Lord, and I am but earth and ashes," "Pray let not my Lord be upset that I speak further," and then again, "Pray let my Lord not be upset that I speak further just this one time."[15] When contemporary lawyers confront judges, they often do the same, prefacing their aggressive arguments with such phrases as "May it please the court" and "We respectfully request." Sometimes when I use such language before particularly contemptible judges, I think of the exchange between Mae West and a judge in the film *My Little Chickadee:*

> Judge: Young lady, are you trying to show contempt for this court?
> Flower Belle Lee: No—I'm doin' my best to hide it.

Let's now consider just how good a lawyer Abraham actually was in his argument with God. Like smart Jewish lawyers and teachers through the ages, he opens with a question—a rhetorical one to be sure, but a question nonetheless. Questions are by their nature interactive; they call for an answer. Of course, in a real trial, God's lawyer would have objected to the question on the ground that it is "compound," because it contains three inquiries plus a combined assertion of facts and opinions. A real judge would sustain the objections and require that each component part be rephrased in the form of a separate question that the witness could answer individually.

So let's break it down. The first question is calculated to secure a factual response, though it is phrased in rather provocative terms: "Will you sweep away the innocent along with the guilty?"

Again the lawyer might object, demanding that the cross-examiner show the court any "basis" he may have for asking such an accusatory question. Abraham would provide two possible bases. The first is God's word itself, stating that He intends to go down and see for Himself whether the reported outrages are true. But God never explicitly threatens to kill the sinners, and certainly not to "sweep away the innocent" along with them. It is Abraham who first raises this dire prospect. So a judge might well reject his first proposed basis for the question as unfounded.

Abraham might then respond as follows:

> Your Honor, remember the last time God saw massive sinning in the world, during the time of my ancestors Noah and Shem. He then

regretted creating human beings, and He swept away the innocent along with the guilty. It is reasonable to infer, therefore, that if God's visit to Sodom confirms the reports of massive evil, He will act in a similar fashion against the entire city. The past is the best predictor of the future, even for a god. He promised never again to bring a *flood*, but He didn't promise not to bring a firestorm. Past is prologue. At the very least, Your Honor, I should be permitted to ask Him whether He once again intends to sweep the innocent along with the guilty.[16]

The judge should be satisfied with this argument and allow Abraham to put the accusatory question to God. Assuming that God was to answer in the affirmative, Abraham would have a basis for his next question, which takes the form of a classic law professor's what-if hypothetical: "What if there should be fifty innocent within the city; will You then wipe out the place and not forgive it for the sake of the fifty innocent who are in it?" Again there would be several objections to this question.

First, it is a hypothetical based on surmise and alleged "facts" that are not in the record on evidence. There is no proof that fifty innocent people, in fact, live in the city. The record shows only the family of Lot arguably fitting that description.[17]

Abraham would then ask the judge to take "judicial notice" of the census figures, which show more than fifty babies and children incapable of sinning. God's lawyer might respond by alleging that his omniscient client knows that babies and children born into a lawless and sinning world will inevitably become sinners when they grow up.[18] But Abraham might point to his ancestor Noah, who was born to sinners and lived among sinners yet was righteous in his generation.

Whichever way the judge was to rule on that objection, there would be a further powerful objection: The question assumes that God's only alternatives are to destroy the entire city, including any innocent people, or to "forgive" the entire city "for the sake of the innocent fifty who are in it." But there is an obvious and logical third alternative: God could destroy only the large number of sinners and spare the fifty (or whatever the number) of innocents. That is what a just system would do. But Abraham, the self-appointed lawyer for the *entire* city, wanted more than justice for the innocent. Like all lawyers, he wanted to win! To paraphrase his own words, he wanted God to sweep the *guilty* along with the innocent—to forgive the sinners "for the sake of the innocent."[19]

On first impression, this may sound illogical, even unjust. Why should guilty sinners who deserve punishment escape their just deserts because there are some innocent people among them? But a deeper analysis suggests that Abraham's "for the sake of" argument fits neatly into God's reason for testing Abraham in the first place. Remember that God told Abraham what He intended to do "so that he may instruct his children and his posterity to keep the way of the Lord by doing what is just and right." Abraham's children and posterity would be fallible humans, not gods. And human justice must take into account the inevitability of human error. Implicit in Abraham's argument is the insight that if a human process of justice results in as many as fifty innocent defendants being falsely condemned, there must be something *systemically* wrong with that process. In our legal system, we refer to this as a "structural" problem or error.

Several American states have acted on Abraham's insight in the context of the death penalty. When the Innocence Project and similar investigative programs demonstrated that numerous innocent people—far more than fifty—had been sentenced to death based on false eyewitness testimony, inaccurate lab tests, questionable fingerprint and voice identifications, and other structural deficiencies, the result was not only to spare the innocent—that obviously *had* to be done[20]—but *also* to spare the possibly guilty "for the sake of" preventing more innocents from being falsely convicted and improperly sentenced to death. No process that produced the death sentence for so many innocent defendants could be *trusted* to distinguish guilt from innocence where lives are at stake.

Abraham's argument, illogical and unjust as it may sound on first impression, continues to resonate to the contemporary ear because our current capital punishment processes continue to threaten to sweep away too many innocents along with the guilty!

Even in the context of imprisonment, we demand proof beyond a reasonable doubt to convict the guilty. We demand this to protect the possibly innocent. This means that some factually guilty will go free "for the sake of" the innocent, thus reflecting the insight of Abraham's argument.

It is also the reason I, and other ethical defense lawyers, are willing to represent defendants who are almost certainly guilty. If we do not, we risk the possibility that innocents will be wrongly convicted. Just as Abraham realized that most of the residents of Sodom—his clients—were guilty, every American criminal lawyer understands that most of his clients are probably guilty. Would anyone want to live in a country in which most criminal defendants were innocent? That might have been true of Stalin's Soviet Union, where the head of the KGB, Lavrenti Beria, told Stalin, "Point me to the man, and I will find the crime." It may still be true in today's Iran, where dissidents are killed without any semblance of justice, or in other countries where defense attorneys are forbidden to defend clients with zeal. It is not true in the United States, which has a long tradition—dating back to John Adams, who defended the British soldiers accused of committing the Boston Massacre—of lawyers zealously defending even the most despised of accused criminals.

The next part of Abraham's compound question is not a question at all; it is a warning—almost a curse!

> "Curse You," or "Profane You," or "How dare You," or "Far be it from You"—to do "such a thing"—"to bring death upon the innocent as well as the guilty, so that the innocent and the guilty fare alike."

> "Objection, Your Honor. There is no question here. It is argument and should be saved for the closing."

> "Sustained. Please ask a question."

So Abraham tries to frame a question. But again, he prefaces it with the same curse-like words: "Chalila l'cha." "Profane are You." This time, he follows it with an ad hominem rhetorical question: "Shall not the Judge of all the earth deal justly?" Because the Bible, in its original Hebrew, does not contain punctuation marks, we can only assume that these words were expressed in question form. In the original Hebrew, it could also take the form of a declarative accusation: "The Judge of all the earth will not do justice!"

Whether a rhetorical question or a declarative statement, the context represents a classic ad hominem argument, juxtaposing God's status as the Judge of all the earth with His apparent willingness to exempt Himself from the universal rules of justice that require differentiation between the guilty and the innocent. Perhaps it would be acceptable for a lesser person to compromise the universal rules of justice, but not for You, God, who hold Yourself out to be the paragon of justice, the Judge of judges, the Legislator of the rules of justice, the Administrator of justice, the Judge of all the earth. Are You above Your own law?

In addition to being an ad hominem argument, it is a classic *a fortiori* argument (or, in the Hebrew, "kal v'chomer"—from easy to more difficult). If mere humans are required to act justly, can God be expected to do anything less?[21]

Despite some technical objections, Abraham's question-arguments are powerful enough to require a reasoned answer from God. This has not always been the case with biblical figures. When Job questioned God's injustice in allowing his innocent children to be killed by Satan in order to test Job's fealty, God rebuked him for even asking:

> Where were you when I laid the foundations for the earth? . . . Do you understand the laws which govern the heavens? . . . Would you go so far as to undermine My judgment, put Me in the wrong so that you might be right? Do you have strength comparable to that of God? Can you, like He, produce the thunder's clap?[22]

But when Abraham issued his far more accusatory challenge, God respectfully offered a reasoned response, treating him as an intellectual and moral equal deserving of the following answer:

> If I find within the city of Sodom fifty innocent ones, I will forgive the whole place for their sake.[23]

God might well have realized that His answer was as hypothetical as the question, because He knew that there were not fifty innocents in Sodom. Or, as a smart lawyer might put it, why argue about a principle when the facts don't support the principle? Or perhaps God was persuaded by Abraham's moral argument, and He accepted the principle without actually knowing whether the facts would show fifty innocents. Recall that God began the discussion by telling us that He had not yet decided whether the outcry was true or false. He was going down to investigate. Maybe He would see a city with a mixture of guilty and innocent. If that's what He finds, then perhaps He should call off the entire enterprise and spare the city.

Now we see the real lawyer at work. Abraham has secured from God a principled agreement—a deal. The principle is that the presence of a certain number of innocents among the numerous sinners of Sodom will result in the "whole place" being spared. Quite a concession. Not only does God recognize it would be unjust to sweep the innocent along with the guilty, but He accepts Abraham's controversial argument that it would be right to sweep the guilty along with the innocent—to save the entire city for the sake of the innocent—*as long as there were enough innocent*. But what constitutes enough—why is fifty a magic number? Why not forty-five? Or forty? So Abraham, the lawyer, begins to do what lawyers do! Negotiate (*hondel* in the Yiddish) with God:

> What if the fifty innocent should lack five? Will You destroy the whole city for want of the five?

It's a clever argument. Now that Abraham has persuaded God to accept the principle, the negotiation is reduced to a numbers game, reminiscent of the somewhat sexist gambit attributed variously to George Bernard Shaw, Winston Churchill, and Groucho Marx:

> A man inquires of a woman whether she would sleep with him for a million dollars. She replies, "Yes." He then asks, "Would you sleep with me for twenty dollars?" The woman replies indignantly, "What kind of woman do you think I am," to which the man counters, "We've already established *that*. Now we're just haggling over the *price*!"

Having established the principle, Abraham was haggling with God over numbers. God agrees that for lack of five He would not destroy the city.

Abraham then lowers the number by five more. Again God accepts:

I will not do it for the sake of the forty.

Now Abraham is on a roll. Thirty? Okay! Twenty? Agreed. Ten? "I will not destroy for the sake of ten." Having won both the principle and a significant reduction from the opening offer of fifty down to ten, some lawyers would have pressed further. Five? Three? Perhaps even one. But Abraham, like other good lawyers, knows when to stop. Having represented to God that his request for ten represented his final negotiation, Abraham "returned to his place," recognizing that God had "finished speaking" to him.[24]

Just as noteworthy as Abraham's decision to step down at the right moment (and waive closing arguments) is the fact that God did not cut him off at any point. Instead, God waited for Abraham to complete his arguments, and only then "He departed." One midrash notes on this verse, "As long as the defense attorney is pleading the case of his client, the judge patiently waits. Only when the defense attorney falls silent is the judge free to go on his way."[25] (Oh, were that the case when I argue before judges who impose rigid time limitations and arbitrarily cut off lawyers in the midst of their arguments!)

Some commentators have taken the position that Abraham's goal was not to save the sinners of Sodom but rather to assure that God had acted justly.[26] So when God agreed to a formula that Abraham believed was just—saving the entire city if there were ten righteous people but saving only the righteous people if there were fewer than ten—Abraham stopped arguing and "returned to his place."

This interpretation is consistent with how *some* defense lawyers see their role—not so much as *seeking to benefit individual defendants*, most of whom are probably guilty, but rather as *defending the system* of justice. I call them "due process lawyers," and I reject their approach. I believe that the *principal* role of the defense lawyer is to help his client, whether innocent or guilty. The overall *effect* of such zealous representation of individual clients may well be to assure that the system as a whole does justice. But if there is a conflict between the principal role and the overall effect, the defense lawyer is duty-bound to prefer the selfish interests of the client (as long as they can be achieved lawfully and ethically) over the altruistic benefits to the system. Nor is this a radical or transient notion. As a British barrister named Henry Brougham put it in 1820:

> An advocate, by the sacred duty which he owes his client, knows, in the discharge of that office, but one person in the world, THAT CLIENT AND NONE OTHER. To save that client by all expedient means,—to protect that client at all hazards and costs to all others, and among others to himself,—is the highest and most unquestioned of his duties; and he must not regard the alarm, the suffering, the torment, the destruction—which he may bring upon any other. Nay, separating even the duties of a patriot from those of an advocate, and casting them, if need be, to the wind, he must go on reckless of the consequences, if his fate it should unhappily be, to involve his country in confusion for his client's protection![27]

It is unclear from the text whether Abraham was a "client-centered" or a "due process" lawyer. His "for the sake of" argument suggests the former, while his "stop at ten" concession suggests the latter.

Abraham's return to "his place" may refer not to a geographic location but to his proper place in relation to God—namely, his "status" as someone who accepts God's superiority over human beings and does not argue with Him, despite His covenant or contract.[28] As we shall soon see, Abraham seems to accept that hierarchical role in a dramatic subsequent encounter with God. But before we go there, let's consider the implications of Abraham's conceptual if Pyrrhic victory over God in his negotiation over numbers.

The very fact that the "Judge of all the earth" would argue about numbers is quite remarkable. In some religious and moral traditions, especially those that reject a cost-benefit utilitarian analysis of moral issues, the life of one person is not to be traded for the lives of others. In the famous if overused "trolley" or train hypothetical, a vehicle on tracks has lost its brakes and will kill five people standing on the track unless the conductor diverts the vehicle onto another track on which one person is standing and will be killed. Though most people say that the conductor should divert and "kill" the one person, thus sparing the five, some argue that killing one to save five is wrong as a matter of principle, because actively killing any innocent human being is always wrong, regardless of the benefit to others.[29]

According to this deontological approach to decision making, numbers don't matter. Killing one innocent is simply and categorically wrong. Dostoyevsky posed that issue in *The Brothers Karamazov* by having Ivan put the ultimate test of relativism to his brother Alyosha:

> "Imagine that you are creating a fabric of human destiny with the object of making men happy in the end, giving them peace and rest at last, but that it was essential and inevitable to torture to death only one tiny creature—that baby beating its breast with its fist, for instance—and to found that edifice on its unavenged tears, would you consent to be the architect on those conditions? Tell me, and tell the truth."
>
> "No, I wouldn't consent," said Alyosha softly.[30]

Maimonides, who was paradoxically both a law-and-order zealot and a compassionate liberal,[31] argued, in support of thorough cross-examinations designed to prevent wrongful convictions in capital cases, that he who takes a single life, it is as if he has destroyed the entire world[32]—thus paraphrasing the famous Talmudic mantra that one who saves a single life, it is as if he has saved the entire world.

The God with whom Abraham negotiated seems to reject this even-one-is-too-much approach. To Him (and to Abraham), sweeping ten innocents along with the many guilty would be too many, but sweeping one or two (or eight or nine) along with the many guilty may be the price that has to be paid for having a viable system of justice. The "benefit" of having such a system outweighs its "costs," if the costs are limited to a small number of innocent people being swept away with the guilty.

Not only did God (and Abraham) accept this cost-benefit approach, but most contemporary democratic legal systems do as well. Every just legal system must recognize the possibility—indeed, the inevitability—of error: some guilty may be wrongly acquitted, while some innocent may be wrongly convicted.[33]

It is easy to assure that no innocent will ever be convicted, if that is the *sole* object. Simply acquit all people about whom there is the slightest doubt as to their guilt, no matter how unreasonable. It is also easy to assure that no guilty person is ever acquitted, if that is the *only* goal. Simply convict everyone against whom there is even the slightest suspicion of guilt, no matter how far-fetched. No system in history has ever managed to convict all the guilty without also sweeping along some innocents. Every rule of evidence or procedure that makes it easier to acquit the innocent—for example, the "two witnesses" rule of the Bible—also makes it easier for some guilty people to escape justice. Likewise, every rule that makes it easier to convict the guilty—for example, current reforms that no longer require "corroboration" of rape accusations—also makes it easier to convict some innocents. The difficult task is to strike the proper balance.[34]

In the end, every system of justice must decide which is worse: convicting *some* innocents or acquitting *some* guilty. Tyrannical regimes always opt for the former: it is far better that many innocents be convicted than that *any* guilty be acquitted (especially if the guilty pose a danger to the regime or its leader). Most just regimes tend to opt for the latter (at least in theory): it is far better that some guilty go free than that innocents be wrongly convicted. This is the approach ultimately accepted in the Bible, with its generally rigorous safeguards for those accused of wrongdoing.[35]

In addition to deciding on this basic preference, every system of justice must quantify—at least implicitly. The Anglo-American system, for example, has proclaimed, "It is better that ten guilty persons escape than that one innocent suffer."[36] That is surely an approximation, but it sends an important message: our preference for not convicting the innocent is a very strong one, but it is not absolute; we acknowledge that in order to convict large numbers of guilty, we will sometimes have to convict an innocent. We will try our best to prevent such an injustice, but we will not simply acquit everyone in order to avoid it. This is the way a mature and just system operates.

The question then arises: How do we decide on the proper numerical ratio?[37] Why did Abraham stop arguing after God agreed to ten? If fifty wasn't a magic number, why is ten? And why does the current American system also use that number when calculating how many convictions of the innocent would be too many to accept? Are the two related?

Traditional commentators have struggled to explain the relevance of the number ten in Abraham's negotiation with God.[38]

My own view is that although ten is an arbitrary number, it seems to reflect an appropriate balance between convicting the innocent and acquitting the guilty. If one does not know the number of wicked people in Sodom, it is impossible, of course, to come up with a precise ratio. But the number ten, even standing alone, is neither trivial nor daunting. Because it is always possible that *any* substantial group of guilty people could include one or two innocents, selecting so low a number would make it impossible to construct a realistic system for convicting the guilty. But tolerating the conviction of more than ten innocents would make any system of convicting the guilty unjust, or at least suspect. When the number of people on Illinois's death row who were freed because of their possible innocence reached double digits, the public began to express concern.[39] Seemingly, the sentencing to death of one or two possibly innocent people was not sufficient to stimulate reconsideration of the death penalty, but once the number climbed beyond ten, even many death penalty advocates began to question whether the system was working fairly. The Anglo-American ratio—better ten guilty go free than even one innocent be wrongly convicted—is also somewhat arbitrary, but it too uses the number ten in attempting to strike the proper balance.

We cannot know for certain whether the ten-to-one ratio in Anglo-American law was derived explicitly from the Abraham narrative or whether both independently reflect a common moral insight about sensible compromise and balance. In any event, this quantification of morality—this negotiation over numbers in the context of teaching about divine and human justice—has resonated with readers of the Bible for millennia and has influenced the way we think about such matters. So Abraham was not only the first Jewish lawyer; he was also the first of many Jewish law teachers.

It is interesting to contrast Abraham's argument with Moses's later confrontation with God in the book of Exodus.[40] Moses goes up to Sinai to receive the tablets, only to learn from God that in his absence the Jewish people have erected a golden calf to worship. God threatens to annihilate this "stiff-necked people" and to make of Moses himself a great nation.

Moses, Abraham's successor at the bar of justice, argues with God in defense of the sinners, pointing out that were God to annihilate the very people He had taken out of Egypt, God would be reneging on His deal with the Israelites, and the Egyptians would rightfully accuse God of having taken them out "with evil intent," only to subsequently kill them here. In other words, Moses appealed not only to God's conscience but also to His vanity and reputation, arguing that if He annihilated the very people He had saved, He would look bad in the eyes of the world. (Such an outcome would have been an ironic example of "chilul Hashem," committed by God Himself!)[41] Moses then invokes God's contract with Abraham and his progeny, reminding the Lord of the promises He had made to the patriarchs. Moses's powerful legal arguments persuade God to change His mind—at least for the moment.

When Moses then descends from Sinai, tablets in hand, to see his people dancing around the golden calf, he destroys both the tablets and the calf. He then has the Levites kill three thousand of the sinners. Realizing that God might once again change His mind, Moses ascends the mountain and again offers a powerful argument in mitigation of the sinners, acknowledging their sins but pleading for forgiveness. In doing so, Moses places his own future on the line: If You refuse to forgive them, then "erase me from Your book that You have written."[42] Commentators interpret this "book" as the book of life.[43] Moses is thus telling God that He can't have it both ways: He can't annihilate the current Jewish population and expect to make a great nation of Moses and his descendants.

God responds very differently from the way He did to Abraham's argument on behalf of the sinners of Sodom. Recall that He had agreed to spare *all* the people of Sodom—including the sinners—if a certain number of righteous people could be found in the city. Now He tells Moses that He will erase from His book *only* those who have sinned. He will not spare the sinners on behalf of the righteous; nor will He annihilate the righteous on account of the sins of the unrighteous. He will do as He has commanded humans to do: individual justice based on individual guilt or innocence. God has learned something about justice from His human legal interlocutors—Abraham and Moses[44]—just as His human interlocutors have learned from Him. Together, Abraham, Moses, and God conducted one heck of a "seminar" on how to achieve human justice in the face of inevitable uncertainty and human failings. We are still learning from this trio of remarkably interactive law teachers.

# 3

Abraham Refuses to Argue with God
and with His Wife over the Lives of His
Children—Failing God's Next Test

After Abraham "returned to his place," God decided to test him—to put him on trial—once again. This time, the stakes were personal. God had already tested Abraham with regard to his concern for strangers. Abraham had aced that exam. Now it was time to test him with regard to his own beloved son.

The story of the Akedah—God's command that Abraham offer up his son Isaac as a sacrifice—has challenged readers and scholars of the Bible for millennia.[1]

Often it is presented as an independent story with no prequel, sequel, or narrative context. Only rarely is it explicitly contrasted with the earlier story of Abraham's argument with God over the sinners of Sodom. This is quite remarkable for several reasons. First, the stories are textually linked. The Akedah narrative begins with an explicit reference to the earlier events: "And it happened *after these events* that God put Abraham to the test." But this was not the first test to which God had put Abraham, and it is only natural that the tests should be seen as related. Indeed, the individual tests—some of which Abraham passed and others of which he failed—are best viewed as part of a larger educational curriculum devised by God the Divine Teacher for His student and messenger Abraham in order to prepare him to "instruct" his progeny to do justice. This series of tests permits God to judge His student's overall performance, in much the same way a professor assigns a final grade following several exams during the course of a semester. A good professor will design different tests to assess different aspects of a student's attributes. (I have always done that with my first-year students at Harvard Law School.) It is all the more surprising, therefore, that so many of the classic Jewish commentators—from ancient midrashim, to Rashi, to Rabbi Samson Raphael Hirsch²—fail to ask the most obvious question: How can one reconcile the confrontational and argumentative Abraham of the Sodom story with the compliant and acquiescing Abraham of the Akedah? Why didn't Abraham once again challenge God when He told Abraham to prepare his innocent son for sacrifice? Why did he not accuse God of profanity in sweeping away yet another innocent, without even the excuse of Isaac's being "collateral damage" in the just cause of sweeping away the guilty? Can this compliant Abraham really be the same man who passed the Sodom test?³ And why do so many traditional commentators, who seek to explain away every minor inconsistency in the text, shy away from taking on one of the greatest apparent inconsistencies in the entire Bible?⁴

Perhaps because they believed that there is no satisfactory way of reconciling the two very different Abrahams. The traditional commentators, like good defense lawyers, rarely ask a question to which they do not have a satisfactory answer. I labor under no such constraints, either as an author or as a lawyer.⁵

It is important, in my view, to relate the various parts of the Abraham narrative to one another. So before we consider the conflict between the Abraham of Sodom and the Abraham of the Akedah, let's turn to the immediate prequel to the near sacrifice of Isaac: the casting out of Abraham's other son Ishmael. The two stories have striking parallels. Abraham's humanity is tested in both stories, and he fails both tests—at least from a humanitarian perspective. In the end, it is God who has to rescue the children from certain and undeserved death.

Sarah, who, as we shall see, is the ultimate victim of the Isaac story, is the villain of the Ishmael story:

Sarah saw the son, whom Hagar the Egyptian had borne to Abraham, playing. She said to Abraham, "Cast out that slave-woman and her son, for the son of that slave shall not share in the inheritance with my son Isaac." The matter distressed Abraham greatly, for it concerned a son of his, and he knew that casting out a mother and child into the wilderness was a likely death sentence. But God said to Abraham, "Do not be distressed over the boy or your slave; whatever Sarah tells you, do as she says, for it is through Isaac that offspring shall be continued for you. As for the son of the slave-woman, I will make a nation of him, too, for he is your seed." Early next morning, Abraham took some bread and a skin of water, and gave them to Hagar. He placed them over her shoulder, together with the child, and sent her away. And she wandered about in the wilderness of Beer-sheba. When the water was gone from the skin, she left the child under the bushes and went and sat down at a distance, a bowshot away, for she thought, "Let me not look on as the child dies." And sitting thus afar, she burst into tears.

God heard the cry of the boy, and an angel of God called to Hagar from heaven and said to her, "What troubles you, Hagar? Fear not, for God has heeded the cry of the boy where he is. Come, lift up the boy and hold him by the hand, for I will make a great nation of him." Then God opened her eyes and she saw a well of water. She went and filled the skin with water, and let the boy drink. God was with the boy and he grew up; he dwelt in the wilderness and became a bowman.

Sarah, who had just fulfilled her dream of bearing a child to Abraham, was jealous of Abraham's son Ishmael, whom she saw was a happy, playful child. Perhaps she was also jealous of Hagar. Like the mothers of so many dynastic children throughout history, Sarah did not want another woman's son to share her son's patrimony and thus elevate the status of his mother. She insisted that Abraham cast out both child and mother. The text makes it clear that Hagar believed that Ishmael's death was a certainty once the water ran out, so she placed him under a bush to shield her eyes from his suffering and death. Abraham's belief is less clear, but at the very least he had to know that he was creating a serious risk of death for his son and his mistress by casting them into the wilderness.

Abraham was thus morally responsible for creating that risk. If he was not guilty of attempted murder as well as conspiracy (along with Sarah) to murder, he was certainly guilty of reckless disregard for life. Why would he do this? Why did he not argue with Sarah about his innocent son as he had argued with God over the sinners of Sodom? The question is not resolved by saying that God told him to do "whatever Sarah tells [him]." He should then have argued with God over *that* immoral directive! But God had said more than just "do what your wife says." He had given a reason: "for it is through Isaac that offspring shall be continued for you." Well, that may satisfy Abraham's need for progeny, but it doesn't excuse his apparent lack of concern for his other child. God responds to that concern as well by assuring Abraham that Ishmael too will become a great nation. In other words, God will somehow assure Ishmael's survival.

So obeying Sarah's immoral order becomes a test of faith. God is saying to Abraham: Look, Sarah may be asking you to do something that appears to be risking Ishmael's life, but don't worry. I have his back. I won't let him die. Trust me. Abraham trusts God. And God comes through. Sarah is happy because her rival and her son's rival have been cast away and won't share the inheritance. Abraham is happy because he hasn't had to get into an argument with his wife, and his other son will remain alive. God is happy because Abraham seems to have placed his trust in God above his understandable concern for his son Ishmael. But God is not completely happy with Sarah, because she seems to have distrusted God's promise that her son, Isaac, will give rise to nations and the covenant will continue through him, not through Ishmael. So she had no reason to be jealous of Ishmael on Isaac's behalf—if she believed God!

But the text is unclear as to whether God ever directly communicated this promise to Sarah, or only to Abraham. And we know how inept husbands can be in communicating messages! Maybe Sarah never learned of God's promise relating to Isaac. We do know from the text that Sarah was skeptical of God's promises. When Sarah overheard God's messengers prophesying that she would bear a son, she "laughed to herself." And then when God asked Abraham, "Why did Sarah laugh?" the text reports that "Sarah denied it, saying 'I did not laugh.'"[6] Abraham the lawyer had trained his client to lie when she was asked whether she was his wife. Lawyers who coach their clients in small deceptions sometimes discover that Sir Walter Scott was correct when he wrote, "Oh! what a tangled web we weave / When first we practise to deceive!"[7]

This strange text forces us to confront the communication conundrum directly: Did God ever talk directly to Sarah? If not, did Abraham communicate God's words to Sarah? Did Sarah overhear them as she did the words of the messengers? Did she know that those men were messengers of God?

The text reports that after Sarah denied laughing, "He replied, 'You did laugh.'" But it is unclear whether "He" refers to Abraham or God. In the context of God's speaking only to Abraham and communicating with Sarah only *through* Abraham, it seems likely that the "He" refers to Abraham (there are no capital letters in the original Hebrew text).[8]

We don't really know, therefore, precisely what Sarah knew about God's promises or whether she distrusted God Himself or only His human interlocutors. The bottom line, however, is that regardless of whether Sarah was aware of God's promise to make a great nation of Isaac, she acted immorally in demanding that Abraham cast away Ishmael and Hagar. We do know that when God later commands Abraham to take Isaac to the mountain and offer him as a burnt sacrifice, nobody—not God, not Abraham nor the servants—tells Sarah of God's immoral order. Indeed, Sarah is never even mentioned in the entire narrative, though she is Isaac's mother and he is her only child.[9] It is as if God were not only testing Abraham but also punishing Sarah for her actions with regard to Ishmael.

Perhaps God also knows that Sarah would try to stop Abraham from obeying His order. She can't be trusted when it comes to Isaac. Moreover, God had previously instructed Abraham to do "whatever Sarah tells you," and Sarah would almost certainly tell him not to sacrifice Isaac. This would complicate the test by introducing cognitive dissonance over conflicting orders from both God and Sarah. It would confuse the test God had devised for Abraham by triangulating the problem: the first angle would be God's command to offer up Isaac; the second angle would be Sarah's counterdemand that God had previously told Abraham to obey; the third would be Abraham's own sense of morality, as manifested in the Sodom story, to prevent the sweeping away of the innocent Isaac.

God apparently preferred a binary test: Obey Me, or obey your own sense of morality. Abraham obeyed God, as the following narrative demonstrates:

Some time afterward, God put Abraham to the test. He said to him, "Abraham," and he answered, "Here I am." And He said, "Take your son, your favored one, Isaac, whom you love, and go to the land of Moriah, and offer him there as a burnt offering on one of the heights which I will point out to you." So early next morning, Abraham saddled his ass and took with him two of his servants and his son Isaac. He split the wood for the burnt offering, and he set out for the place of which God had told him. On the third day Abraham looked up and saw the place from afar. Then Abraham said to his servants, "You stay here with the ass. The boy and I will go up there; we will worship and we will return to you."

Abraham took the wood for the burnt offering and put it on his son Isaac. He himself took the firestone and the knife; and the two walked off together. Then Isaac said to his father Abraham, "Father!" And he answered, "Yes, my son." And he said, "Here are the firestone and the wood; but where is the sheep for the burnt offering?" And Abraham said, "God will see to the sheep for His burnt offering, my son." And the two of them walked on together. They arrived at the place of which God had told him. Abraham built an altar there; he laid out the wood; he bound his son Isaac; he laid him on the altar, on top of the wood.

And Abraham picked up the knife to slay his son. Then an angel of the Lord called to him from heaven: "Abraham! Abraham!" And he answered, "Here I am." And he said, "Do not raise your hand against the boy, or do anything to him. For now I know that you fear God, since you have not withheld your son, your favored one, from Me."[10]

And so we return to the critical question of why Abraham didn't employ his considerable legal acumen and argumentative skills once again to argue with God, this time about his innocent son Isaac.

One obvious answer, deriving directly from the Ishmael story, is that Abraham knew that God had repeatedly promised him that Isaac would be the progenitor of a great nation, and therefore God was bluffing—the test was a simple one to pass. All he had to do was go through the motions of "offering" his son up as a sacrifice. He knew God would never accept the "offer," for to do so would require Him to break His promise.[11] And God had already shown that He doesn't break His promises when He rescued Ishmael from apparent death at the last minute.[12] If He rescued Ishmael, then a fortiori (*kal v'chomer*) He would certainly rescue Isaac, with regard to whom He had made a far more important promise. If this was the case, then the test was not a particularly daunting one, because Abraham was certain of the result.[13] Moreover, Abraham could control the outcome. (This is one of the criteria for distinguishing mere preparation from criminal attempt.) If God didn't come through at the last minute, Abraham could always abort the mission, because it was he, Abraham, who controlled whether Isaac would live or die (unlike with Ishmael).[14] If God was to break His promise, why should Abraham keep his? Quid pro quo. That's what a contract is all about. Perhaps that's the reason some commentators, particularly in the Christian tradition, alter the story a bit and have Abraham actually kill Isaac, only to have God restore him to life, as according to Christian theology He did Jesus.[15] Now, *that* would be a test of faith!

The traditional interpretation of the Akedah—in Jewish, Christian, and Islamic theology—is that Abraham proves his faith in God and in God's justice by his willingness to accept God's terrible command.[16] Fair enough! But then why didn't Abraham, the man of faith, have faith that God would never sweep the innocent along with the guilty of Sodom? Why did he have so little faith in God's justice that he was prepared to curse Him (even conditionally) as one who might not do justice, despite His status as Judge of the entire earth? One possible answer is that Abraham didn't have faith in God's justice *before* the denouement of the Sodom story, because prior to that God had shown much injustice by destroying nearly all of mankind in the Flood. But Abraham trusted God *after* Sodom because he saw that God had acted justly toward the Sodomites. But in the absence of a persuasive distinction, the doubting Abraham of Sodom is not easily reconcilable with the faithful Abraham of the Akedah.

Indeed, the great philosopher Immanuel Kant imagines an Abraham who resists God's immoral command to sacrifice his innocent son, just as he resists God's immoral intention to sweep the innocents of Sodom along with the guilty. Here is what Kant would have had Abraham say to God: "That I ought not to kill my good son is quite certain. But that you, this apparition [who ordered me to do so] are God—of that I am not certain."[17] Woody Allen paraphrased Kant in his book *Without Feathers:*

> God: How could thou doest such a thing?
> Abraham: But thou said—
> God: Never mind what I said. Dost thou listen to every crazy idea that cometh thy way? . . .
> Abraham: See, I never know when you're kidding.[18]

(Bob Dylan expressed this idea more succinctly in a song: "God said to Abraham, 'Kill me a son.'/Abe says, 'Man, you must be puttin' me on.'")[19]

Acceding to an irrational command might show an Abraham of faith—faith that an actual moral God would not command so immoral a deed. If this is the case, then we see in the Abraham of the Akedah the first Jewish fundamentalist. To borrow the words Søren Kierkegaard applied to a fictional character, we see a man who "was no thinker, he felt no need to go further than faith."[20] Or, in terms more familiar to lawyers, we see Abraham as the first "originalist" or "literal interpreter" of authoritative texts. What, after all, could be more "original" or "authoritative" than a direct command from God Himself? What right does a mere mortal have to question such a divine order, which is so clear on its face? Divine positive law must prevail over the natural feelings of a father.

The question of whether a direct word from God has hierarchical superiority to the written law and its authoritative interpretation has been debated in Jewish tradition. The Talmud recounts a controversy in which the great rabbi Eliezer was engaged in an acrimonious dispute with the other sages about an arcane point of law. Eliezer was certain that his interpretation of the Torah was the correct one, and he "brought forward every imaginable argument, but they did not accept them." Finally, in desperation, he invoked the original intent of the author of the Torah, God Himself. Eliezer implored, "If the halachah [the authoritative meaning of the law] agrees with me, let it be proved from Heaven!"—whereupon a heavenly voice cried out to the others, "Why do ye dispute with R[abbi] Eliezer, seeing that . . . the halachah agrees with him!" (Pretty authoritative evidence of the original intent!) But another of the rabbis rose up and rebuked God for interfering in this very human dispute: "Thou has long since written in the Torah," and "we pay no attention to a Heavenly Voice." The message was clear: God's children were telling their Father, "It is our job, as the rabbis, to give meaning to the Torah that You gave us. You gave us a document to interpret, and a methodology for interpreting it. Now leave us to do our job." God agreed, laughing with joy, "My . . . [children] have defeated Me in argument."[21] The Abraham story takes place, of course, before the Torah was given, so perhaps God's voice had hierarchical superiority at that time.[22]

It is paradoxical that the Abraham of the Sodom story is the world's first defense lawyer willing to challenge God's justice, while the Abraham of the Akedah is the world's first Jewish fundamentalist—a man who elevates faith over morality, fundamentalism over reason. Kierkegaard denominates Abraham a "knight of faith."[23] When God demands "proof of his faith"—when He places Abraham "on trial"—He demands "teleological suspension of the ethical."[24] He insists that Abraham stop thinking, doubting, and questioning, as he had done during the Sodom episode. Abraham had proved his capacity and his willingness to elevate morality and reason over respect for the divine *when invited to do so by God.*[25] His intelligence and chutzpah were thus beyond doubt. Now it was time for God to test his faith—to see whether he was prepared to suspend the universal justice that forbids punishing the innocent and the universal morality that demands love of one's child and to act on blind faith in God's command.[26] Kierkegaard the existentialist suggests that Abraham was ordered to act "on the strength of the absurd; for it is precisely the absurd that as the single individual he is higher than the universal."[27]

Jesus demanded a similar show of unnatural and absurd faith when, according to Luke, he too demanded that his disciples place duty to God over love for the natural objects of their affection:

> If any man come to me and hate not his father, and mother, and wife, and children and brethren and sisters, yea, and his own life also, he cannot be my disciple.[28]

There is, of course, an enormous difference between *hating* one's child and *sacrificing* him—especially if you love him—but both demand that duty to God be elevated over love for family and that faith be placed above reason and morality. The verse from 1 Corinthians 4:10 suggests a similar hierarchy when it says "We are fools for Christ."[29]

This is the essence of fundamentalism, if it is interpreted to require the suspension of reason, natural feelings, and universal morality in order for the believer to prevail in a trial of faith and to be blessed as a knight of faith. This is what Abraham did when his faith was placed on trial by God and he resisted the temptation to act in accord with his moral and filial obligation to save his son. A midrash has Abraham telling God, after the fact, "I suppressed my feelings of pity in order to do thy will."[30] And there is some textual support for the proposition that God tested Abraham by pitting his *love* for Isaac against his *faith* in God. When God first asks Abraham to offer his son as a sacrifice, He describes Isaac as "your son, your favored one, Isaac, *whom you love*." But after Abraham lifts his knife to obey God's command, the angel, in describing Isaac, *omits the words "whom you love"*: "You have not withheld your son, your favored one, from Me." Abraham had passed the test of faith by placing it above his love for Isaac. Faith won. Love lost. Abraham was no longer entitled to have Isaac described as the son "whom you love."

One medieval rabbinic commentator reduces Abraham's difficult decision to sacrifice his beloved son into a simple cost-benefit calculation by ascribing to Abraham knowledge of a world to come, where he would be repaid:

> It shows that our forefathers presupposed the existence of another world beyond this one. If not for Avraham's belief in *olam haba* [the world to come], he certainly would not have agreed to sacrifice his only son and continue living a life without hope and without a future. He was ready to listen to Hashem's [God's] commandment, knowing that for his sacrifice in this world, Hashem would repay him well in *olam haba*.[31]

But there is no textual support for this overly simplistic interpretation that turns the excruciating moral dilemma into a crass betting parlor. The trial of the Akedah was all the more daunting if Abraham did not expect an afterlife in which he would be reunited with his beloved son or rewarded for sacrificing him. As Kierkegaard saw it,

> But Abraham had faith, and had faith for *this* life. Yes, had his faith only been for a future life it would indeed have been easier to cast everything aside in order to hasten out of this world to which he did not belong.[32]

It is informative to contrast Abraham's decision to sacrifice his son's life with Saint Thomas More's decision to sacrifice his own life. More—who did believe in an afterlife—calculated the costs and benefits of dying for his faith. More, whose decision to become a martyr to defend Catholicism has sometimes been compared to Abraham's decision to sacrifice his son, lived in a very different theological world,[33] a world in which earthly sacrifices were rewarded in heaven and earthly sins were punished in hell.[34]

Though More acknowledged that he feared physical pain, he feared it far less than eternal damnation. He wrote to a friend that his was "a case in which a man may lose his head and yet have none harm."[35]

This is the conundrum of religious martyrdom for zealots who believe in reward and punishment in an afterlife. Religious leaders who select martyrs and saints cannot have it both ways. They cannot declare such a believer to be both a hero and a saint, because the two honors are logically inconsistent. To the extent one is an undoubting believer, he is less of a hero for choosing death over eternal damnation. To the extent he is a real hero, he is necessarily less of an undoubting believer. Real heroes are those who face death for a principle—say, to save the lives of others—without any promise of reward in the hereafter.

We do not know enough about the real Thomas More—as distinguished from the mythical "Man for All Seasons," popularized in the play and the film, who was sanctified both for his heroism and for his belief without any overt recognition of the inherent conflict—to decide on which end of the continuum he justly belongs.[36]

If More really expected no harm and great benefit in the hereafter—including sainthood—then his actions were closer to the prudential than to the heroic.

The same cannot be said about Abraham, who expected great harm—the death of his child—with no reward in the afterlife. What, then, was Abraham's reason for obeying God's immoral command? Was it *fear* of a more powerful being? Was it *expectation* of earthly reward from that powerful being? Was it out of a sense of *duty*? Blind faith? Unquestioning love of God?

Maimonides refuses to attribute Abraham's compliance to simple fear of consequences: "For Abraham did not hasten to kill Isaac out of fear that God might slay him or make him poor, but solely because it is man's duty to love and to fear God, even without hope of reward or fear of punishment."[37] But why, then, is Judaism (as well as other religions) so premised on reward and punishment, both in this world and in those to come? True morality can best be judged in the absence of threats or promises. The atheist who throws himself in front of a car to save a child is performing a truly moral act, because he expects no reward. The religious person who strongly believes that he will be rewarded for his moral acts and punished for his immoral ones may simply be making a cost-benefit wager. The fallacy inherent in Pascal's wager—a fallacy pointed out by Jefferson[38]—is that a good God may despise those who engage in such self-serving wagers and prefer those who honestly doubt or even disbelieve. Maimonides argued strongly against the midrashic variation of Pascal's wager:

> Let not a man say, "I will observe the precepts of the Torah and occupy myself with its wisdom in order that I may obtain all the blessings written in the Torah, or to attain life in the world to come; I will abstain from transgressions against which the Torah warns, so that I may be saved from the curses written in the Torah, or that I may not be cut off from life in the world to come." It is not right to serve God after this fashion, for whoever does so, serves Him out of fear. This is not the standard set by the prophets and sages.[39]

Even the noble motive attributed to Abraham by Maimonides and other commentators—duty to love, obey, and fear God—is somewhat self-serving. Abraham placed his allegiance to the all-powerful God above his obligation as a parent, a husband, and a moral human being. Tragically, many Jewish lawyers throughout history have made similar choices when authority has commanded immorality.

What, then, is the nature of God's test of Abraham? The best evidence of that comes from the mouth of God's own angel, who declares that Abraham passed the test: "Now I know that you are in awe of God." The actual Hebrew word is *y'rei*, which literally means "afraid of" or "in fear of" God. The Vilna Gaon, the leading eighteenth-century Lithuanian rabbinic scholar, interprets this statement to mean that until this instance, Abraham had proven himself to be compassionate. During the Akedah, however, he showed himself to be capable of mercilessness (*achzariut*) as well—when God so commands.[40] The Gaon explains that when an individual is observed to possess only one kind of positive character trait (such as compassion) to an exemplary degree, that individual might just be naturally so inclined; when that person also demonstrates an opposing trait, however, it becomes clear that he has striven to attain character perfection.[41] But what kind of a moral test is it to accede to God's command to show immoral mercilessness? Acceding to an immoral command out of fear does not show much courage or virtue. What if a powerful human king had presented Abraham with a similar terrible choice: "Either kill your child or I will kill you"? Would we praise a father for being "afraid of" the king or being "in awe of" the king and killing the child? Of course not. At most, we might understand why the father, like those parents during the Holocaust who abandoned or even sacrificed their crying children, might have made such a decision. We might even feel uncomfortable condemning him. But we would hardly praise him the way we would a father who placed his own life at risk to save his child. Why, then, do we praise Abraham? He might have passed God's test of faith, fear, and duty, but at the moral cost of failing his own test of justice as he articulated it during his argument over the condemned of Sodom— namely, that it is always wrong to kill the innocent, even if it is God who demands such immorality.[42]

When the Judge of all the earth contemplates doing injustice, it is the duty of a moral person to resist that injustice, as Abraham did with regard to Sodom, even if resistance displeases his God. So unless Abraham believed that God would never allow him to carry out the command to sacrifice Isaac, he should have resisted or at least challenged God's immoral demand and failed the test of faith.

A possible alternative interpretation, but one that finds little direct textual support, is that although God *believed* He was testing Abraham, in reality Abraham was testing God. If so, this was Abraham's second test of God, the first being his challenge regarding Sodom, which God passed. Under this theory, Abraham would never have plunged the knife into his innocent son. He knew that God was testing him to see how far he would go. But Abraham was also testing God to see how far *He* would go. If God didn't stop Abraham at the last possible moment, Abraham would have stopped himself. After all, he—Abraham—had to make the final decision to kill or not to kill. He would not obey—or accept—a God who would actually permit him to sacrifice his son. So this was the ultimate game of chicken. Who would back down first? Both passed the test: Abraham by showing God that he was prepared to obey his command (though he really wasn't); God by showing Abraham that He did not really want Isaac to be sacrificed (although he apparently wanted Abraham to believe He did).

The theory, of course, contemplates a God—or at least an angel—who can be, and was, fooled into thinking that Abraham would have gone through with the sacrifice unless he was stopped.

> For now I know that you fear God, since you have not withheld your son, your favored one, from Me.

The real test, and the one suggested by some Christian sources, would have been for God to wait until *after* Abraham had plunged the knife into Isaac before pronouncing that Abraham had passed the test of faith. But the Abraham of the above theory might have failed *that* test. And so would God.

In the Jewish tradition, nearly all mainstream commentators stick to the letter of the text whereby Abraham raises his arm in preparing to slaughter Isaac and is stopped only by the words of the angel.[43] In other words, he engaged in what the law regards as "preparation" or "attempt" to commit murder. Whether Abraham's act crosses the line from non-criminal preparation to criminal attempt depends on a variety of factors beyond the knowledge of the reader of the text.

At the moment the angel interceded, had Abraham formed a firm intention to kill, or had he not yet made up his mind? Would he have actually gone through with the dastardly act had the angel not timely intervened? (The angel certainly thought so!) What exactly do the somewhat ambiguous words tell us about Abraham's precise arm movements? Did he merely raise his arm? Did he begin to lower it toward Isaac?[44] What was the look in his eyes?[45] Did he say anything to Isaac? Did Isaac believe he was about to be killed?[46] Did Abraham intend for Isaac to so believe?[47] What, if anything, did Isaac say to his father on the way home? Did the blade actually touch Isaac's skin and draw blood before the angel ordered him to stop?[48]

I have had cases like this in my practice, and the outcomes have been fact-specific. In one such case, the defendant was holding a knife above his victim when the police burst into the room demanding—much like the angel—that he drop it, which he did. He claimed that he intended to frighten—not kill—the victim. The prosecution argued that he intended to kill and would have but for the unanticipated intervention of the police. On appeal, I cited the Abraham story and argued that we could not know with any degree of certainty, and surely not beyond a reasonable doubt, what was in the defendant's mind and whether he, like Abraham, would actually have killed were it not for the intervention of a deus ex machina—an outside force.

We won the case on other grounds, and it was never retried, so we don't know how the courts would have decided the perplexing "Abraham issue."

Nor do we know what happened between Abraham and Isaac, or between Abraham and Sarah, after the angel interceded. Wouldn't you like to have been a fly on the wall during the walk down from the mountain and when Abraham got home and his wife asked him, "Where have you been, Abe?"

The biblical narrative not only denies us knowledge of any substantive conversation between Isaac and Abraham following the Akedah but tells us that "Abraham then returned to his servants." There is no mention of Isaac. What happened to the boy? Where did he go when his father returned to his servants? Was Abraham alone when he returned to them? Why is Isaac not mentioned? This poignant omission has fueled speculation by the commentators, ranging from God's taking Isaac to the Garden of Eden so he could recover from the trauma of nearly being killed by his father,[49] to Abraham's sending Isaac away to learn Torah,[50] to Abraham's sending Isaac down separately at night so as to avoid any "ayin harah" (evil eye) from the other attendants,[51] to an allegorical interpretation in which God considered it *as if* Isaac's ashes had been placed on the altar.[52]

As to Sarah, not only do we not know what she might have said to her husband, but we don't even know whether she ever again spoke. The next thing the Bible says about her is that she died at age 127 and Abraham mourned her and bought a burial site for her near Hebron.[53]

Nor is there any direct evidence from the biblical narrative that Abraham and Isaac ever spoke to each other again.[54] Abraham did not even bless Isaac before he "breathed his last" as other patriarchs would famously bless their sons.[55] Indeed, the Bible says that "after the death of Abraham, *God* blessed his son Isaac," strongly implying that Abraham—although he "willed all that he owned to Isaac"—never blessed him.[56]

It remains for us to speculate about the nature of Abraham's face-to-face relationships—if any—with the son he seemed willing to kill and with the child's mother, from whom he apparently withheld his homicidal intention.[57]

Abraham was kinder to Sarah after her death[58] and to Isaac after Abraham's own death than he was when they were all alive following the obvious trauma of the aborted sacrifice. Excessive devotion to God takes a toll on familial relationships. Joseph Story once quipped that law "is a jealous mistress."[59] So is religion.

If Abraham passed the test of faith but failed the test of morality by his willingness to sacrifice his beloved son, God has surely failed His own test throughout history, during which millions of Jewish children have been sacrificed without God's intervening to save them as He saved Ishmael and Isaac. Neither Ishmael nor Isaac volunteered to become a martyr; they were chosen. It is not even clear whether they were aware that they had been selected for sacrifice. In both cases, God sent an angel to prevent the killing, thus sending a message that He would intervene again if He was again to ask parents to prove their faith by offering up their children. But this has proved to be a false message. Over and over again, Jewish children have been offered up in the name of "kiddush Hashem"—the holiness of God. And over and over again, God has failed to intervene. He has even been placed "on trial" for His breach of the covenant.[60] He should have pleaded guilty, perhaps with an explanation, but even a creative defense lawyer would have a difficult time coming up with a convincing explanation for why God is prepared to test parents by asking them to sacrifice their children and then fails His own test of morality by allowing these innocent children to die.

It can be argued that God is simply cautioning His chosen people that among the fates He has chosen them to endure are His own imperfections—His temper tantrums and immorally disproportionate reactions to human failings. This is a far more satisfying interpretation than the traditional ones offered by defensive commentators and by God Himself in his interaction with Job: namely, that mere human beings cannot be expected to understand and second-guess God's "justice"—as if any concept of justice, divine or human, could encompass tragedies such as the Crusades or the Holocaust. God's ways may be mysterious, but no mystery can justify what God has allowed to be done to innocent children throughout history.

The late scholar and teacher David Hartman cites three biblical accounts that demonstrate God's failure to respond meaningfully to Abraham's rhetorical challenge in the Sodom story, showing that "the Judge of all the earth will not Himself do justice."[61]

Now Nadav and Avihu, the sons of Aaron, took their respective fire pans, and after putting fire in them, placed incense on it and offered strange fire before the Lord, which He had not commanded them. And fire came out from the presence of the Lord and consumed them, and they died before the Lord. (Leviticus 10:1–2, 6)

And the Lord struck down the men of Beit Shemesh because they had looked into the ark of the Lord, striking down of the people 50,070 men, and the people mourned because the Lord had struck the people with a great slaughter. (1 Samuel 6:19)

But when they came to the threshing floor of Nakhon, Uzzah reached out toward the ark of the Lord, and took hold of it, for the oxen nearly upset it. And the anger of the Lord burned against Uzzah, and God struck him down there for his error and he died there by the ark of God. (2 Samuel 6:6)

In each of these instances—and in others—God acts in ways that are inconsistent with the rules of justice and proportionality that He has ordained for human beings. Perhaps the message of the Akedah and Sodom stories is do not expect justice—at least justice as understood by humans—to come from God. Human justice must come from human beings.

I try to make that point when I argue to juries. I tell them the story of the revered Hasidic rabbi who had a reputation for never saying anything negative about any person or group. His students decided to challenge this man of God by asking him to say something positive about atheists. The rabbi responded, "When you see a poor person begging for food, become an atheist." The students, in shock, asked, "Why?" The rabbi told them, "Because God will not feed him. Only *you* can save his life." I tell the jurors that they too cannot count on God's justice. "Only you can do justice and save the life of an innocent person."

In the Sodom story, God taught Abraham a lesson about the quest for, and limitations of, human justice. In the Akedah and subsequent stories, God taught Abraham not to rely on God's justice, because sometimes the angel will intervene and sometimes it won't.

One modern commentator on the Akedah, Shalom Spiegel, wonders why the power of the Abraham-Isaac story has not been "diminished" by the far greater sacrifices that many Jews have had to make over the millennia. As he put it in his book *The Last Trial*,

> Who cares about some ancient, far off in time, who was merely *thought of as a possible* sacrifice on the altar, but who was delivered from the danger, whom no misfortune overtook; when right before your eyes, in the immediate present, fathers and sons *en masse* ascend the executioner's block to be butchered and burned, literally butchered and burned?[62]

Spiegel was referring specifically to the Crusades, during which many fathers were forced to sacrifice their sons. He contrasts the following tragic story of an "unbound" son with the near sacrifice of the bound Isaac:

> Now there was a certain saintly man there, an elder well on in years, and his name was Rabbenu Samuel bar Yehiel. He had an only son, a splendid looking young man, who with his father fled into the water

and there offered his throat for slaughter by his father. Whereupon the father recited the appropriate blessing for the slaughter of cattle and fowl, and the son responded with "Amen." And all those who were standing around them responded in a loud voice, "Hear, O Israel, the Lord our God, the Lord is One." O citizens of the world, take a good look! How extraordinary was the stamina of the son who *unbound* let himself be slaughtered, and how extraordinary was the stamina of the father who could resist compassion for an *only son*, so splendid and handsome a young man. Can anyone hear of this and remain dry-eyed?[63]

He then marvels at the fact that the victims of the barbaric Crusades[64] never protested that their sacrifices were greater than Abraham's:

It is all the more amazing to read countless times in the contemporary sources that both the sacrificers and the very victims of sacrifice saw as the crowning act of their role the performance of the Fathers Abraham and Isaac, as though no trial could be greater than that endured by the Patriarchs. . . . They too offered up their sons, *exactly* as Abraham offered up his son Isaac. . . . There were 1,100 victims in one day, every one of them like the *Akedah of Isaac son of Abraham*. . . .

Like a permanent refrain, this comparison of their experience with that of the Patriarchs recurs in all the writings of that generation . . . :

*They offered up sacrifices, they prepared victims* like Isaac their Father.

Like Isaac their Father? But was not Isaac delivered from the knife's thrust? Was he not restored to his father very much alive? These pious folk were butchered and became food for the worms! How is it then that from out of the mouths of these votaries and victims, or the relations of the slain, there did not burst forth a painful groan like to that of the saintly mother, bereft of all her sons, as she addressed herself to Father Abraham and, even more, to the deaf-mute heavens—"You built one altar and *did not* sacrifice your son, but we built altars in the hundreds and thousands and *did sacrifice* our children on them! Yours was the *trial*, but ours were the *performances*!"

Not a hint of this; not a whisper of such thoughts in the records of those times. You will never find that they protest: How compare the one who gave his life to the one who did not have to do so?[65]

During the Holocaust, there were many more stories of even greater sacrifices. The Nobel Peace Prize laureate and concentration camp survivor Elie Wiesel has noted that the Hebrew term *olah*—typically translated as "burnt offering"—more accurately means "an offering that has been totally consumed, a holocaust."[66] In his book *Messengers of God*, Wiesel confesses that he has "always felt much closer to Isaac than to his father, Abraham."[67] He writes further,

> Of all the Biblical tales, the one about Isaac is perhaps the most timeless and most relevant to our generation. We have known Jews who, like Abraham, witnessed the death of their children; who, like Isaac, lived the *Akeda* in their flesh; and some who went mad when they saw their father disappear on the altar, with the altar, in a blazing fire whose flames reached into the highest of heavens.
>
> We have known Jews—ageless Jews—who wished to become blind for having seen God and man opposing one another in the invisible sanctuary of the celestial spheres, a sanctuary illuminated by the gigantic flames of the holocaust. . . .
>
> Isaac survived; he had no choice. He had to make something of his memories, his experience, in order to force us to hope.
>
> For our survival is linked to his. . . . Isaac too represents defiance. Abraham defied God [regarding Sodom], Isaac defied death.[68]

Wiesel then ponders why "the most tragic of our ancestors was named Isaac, a name which evokes and signifies laughter."[69] He suggests the following explanation:

> As the first survivor, he had to teach us, the future survivors of Jewish history, that it is possible to suffer and despair an entire lifetime and still not give up the art of laughter.
>
> Isaac, of course, never freed himself from the traumatizing scenes that violated his youth; the holocaust had marked him and contin-

ued to haunt him forever. Yet he remained capable of laughter. And in spite of everything, he did laugh.[70]

Even now, as our collective, vivid image of the Holocaust slowly evolves into a distant memory—the trial of a previous generation—the Akedah story remains poignantly relevant. Today, as Israel faces threats both external and internal, Israeli fathers and mothers hear a voice commanding them to bring their eighteen-year-old sons, and now their daughters, to the mountaintop where they will face possible death from Israel's enemies.

It is precisely because the Jewish people have faced so many sacrificial demands that the story of the Akedah, even though it has a relatively happy ending, continues to resonate, especially with people who have experienced so much persecution. The power of the Akedah has not in fact diminished over time. It has retained its power to make us all ponder what we would do if faced with a horrible choice involving the lives of our children.[71]

The story of the Akedah—especially when read against the backdrop of the Sodom story—also makes us think about the contemporary issue of religious fundamentalism, which leads people to do terrible things because their God has allegedly commanded it. Some Islamic fundamentalists engage in suicide bombings in the name of jihad. Some Jewish fundamentalists devalue the lives of non-Jews because they believe this is God's will.[72] Some Christian fundamentalists elevate the life of a fetus over that of the mother because God ordained it.

The conflict between obeying God's literal word—or the words of those who are authorized to interpret it—and listening to one's own conscience is inherent in every religion that is based on belief in God. This conflict is played out dramatically in the conflict between the Akedah and Sodom. God's command prevails over Abraham's morality in the Akedah, whereas Abraham's morality prevails in Sodom. There are other evidences of this inherent conflict in other parts of the Torah. In Deuteronomy, for example, God orders Moses to "engage" the king of Heshbon "in battle," even though his kingdom was merely on the way to the promised land and not a part of it. Moses disobeys God's order and tries instead to find a peaceful resolution:

> Then I sent messengers with an offer of peace, as follows, "Let me pass through your country. I will keep strictly to the highway, turning off neither to the right nor to the left. What food I eat you will supply for money, and what water I drink you will furnish for money: just let me pass through . . . [t]hat I may cross the Jordan into the land that the Lord our God is giving to us."[73]

In the end, Moses's peaceful approach fails, because the king refuses to let the Israelites pass through. According to Midrash Rabbah, Moses, by disobeying God's order, caused Him to change His mind:

> God replied: "By your life. I will cancel my opinion [literal translation] and follow yours,["] as it states [later in Deuteronomy 20:10] "when you approach a town to attack it, you shall offer it terms of peace."

The result of this interaction between God and Moses was to create a "new legal paradigm for morality of war."[74]

According to this view, best expressed by the modern commentator Donniel Hartman, the Sodom and Akedah stories cannot be reconciled, precisely because they represent strains of Jewish (indeed religious) tradition that are ultimately irreconcilable:

> The diversity of opinions present in the Jewish tradition on this issue reflects two very distinct and often incompatible religious instincts. We tread on superficial ground when we attempt to discount either the validity or religious sensitivity of either. In many ways, this may be [the] deepest intent of the Bible when it has Abraham embody both. There is the Abraham of Genesis 18 and the Abraham of Genesis 22. They are both present, both equally representative of the will of God.
>
> The presence of both positions, however, has profound practical implications. As stated above, this debate is not merely a theoreti-

cal, theological one regarding the nature of divinity, but an issue which determines the direction and meaning of religious life. Each approach not only reflects a different religious sensibility, but also generates different moral responses. How religion will respond to the moral challenges of modernity will be determined in no small measure [by] which Abraham personifies one's religious ideal.[75]

If "a foolish consistency is the hobgoblin of little minds," as Emerson quipped,[76] then a singular approach to interpreting the Bible in general or Abraham in particular is also small-minded. So now let us conclude the Abraham narrative.

# 4

---

# Abraham Negotiates to Buy
# a Burial Cave for Sarah

Following Sarah's death in Kiryat Arba (currently part of the city of Hebron), Abraham "came to eulogize Sarah and to weep for her." This construction suggests that he was not with her at her time of death, thus lending corroboration to the theory that they separated following the trauma of the Akedah.[1] Nor is there any mention of Isaac's being with his mother either before or after she died—even when she was eulogized and buried. Abraham apparently sat a form of shiva,[2] because the Bible says that he "rose up [*vayakam*] from the presence of his dead," but there is no reference to Isaac's sitting with him.

Whatever the family dynamic when Sarah died, her widower decided to secure an appropriate burial site for her, selecting the Cave of Machpelah on the edge of the property of a man named Ephron, son of Zohar. The apparently generous Ephron offered his neighbor the cave and the surrounding fields as a gift,[3] but Abraham insisted on paying its full value of four hundred silver shekels so that "the children of Heth"—the surrounding neighbors—would see that a contract had been agreed to and that Abraham owned the cave and the fields around it.[4]

The Jews who now live in Hebron cite this biblical account in support of this area being part of the Jewish patrimony. They see Abraham as a farsighted real estate lawyer who realized that the value of the land would increase and that if it was to become the object of controversy, a binding contract, with fair monetary consideration, would be more persuasive than a mere gift. Hence Abraham was the first, but certainly not the last, shrewd Jewish real estate lawyer who understood the value of "location."

Moreover, he provided a model that Jewish leaders would follow in establishing the modern State of Israel. The early Zionists bought the land they cultivated from Arab landowners, many of them absentees living in Lebanon and Syria. They paid fair, sometimes "too fair," prices, and they registered their land purchases with the authorities, as Abraham essentially did by purchasing his land in full view of the neighbors, making certain that all the legal niceties were satisfied, as any good lawyer would do.

## Summarizing Abraham's Development: From Radical Idol Smasher to Conservative Real Estate Developer

We see Abraham in many different lights through these narratives: an idol smasher, a conniver, a rescuer, an advocate, a compliant fundamentalist, and a shrewd real estate investor. In this regard, Abraham's development over time reflects the quip variously attributed to Winston Churchill, John Adams, and other wits: "Show me a young conservative, and I'll show you someone with no heart. Show me an old liberal, and I'll show you someone with no brain."[5] The young Abraham is a radical civil disobedient, disrespectful of his father, with few ties to home, family, nation, or law. As he gets older, he becomes more logical, more committed to respectful if forceful dialogue, and more protective of his wife and nephew. Having achieved the respect of his powerful God, Abraham savors his position and blindly accepts God's immoral command, elevating authority over morality. Finally, as he approaches mortality, he seeks the stability of an eternal resting place for his wife and himself—purchasing real property that will endure forever.

Viewed in this way, Abraham's life becomes a metaphor for the development of many Jewish lawyers, if not humans in general. These are the Abrahamic characteristics on which I shall focus in my effort to relate the actions of the world's first Jewish lawyer to those of the many who followed him throughout the annals of history. As we shall see, Abraham's acts and omissions—as interpreted by Jewish, Christian, Muslim, and secular commentators—have adumbrated both the positive and the negative roles of Jewish and other lawyers who have followed in the steps of his very large sandals.

# PART II

---

In the Footsteps of Abraham:
Jews on Trial,
as Defendants and Defenders

# INTRODUCTION

The fascination, if not the obsession, that Jews have had with law and justice over the millennia cannot be fully understood on the basis of books alone, even books as powerful and law centered as the Torah, the Talmud, the Midrash, and the commentaries and codifications. For books to remain a vibrant source of inspiration, their content must have continuing relevance and influence on the lives of those who read and live by their words. Words without experience become dead letters, just as experience without words becomes acts without meaning.

The long experience Jews have had with persecution has brought the sacred words of the scriptures to life—and, all too often, to death. Jews have come to appreciate justice and the rule of law because we have experienced so much injustice and the rule of might over right. We have been on trial throughout our history, and the trials have more often been unfair than just. We have struggled for the rule of law and the reality of justice both because they are abstractly right and because we have needed them to survive and thrive.

From the beginning of Jewish history, the trial, both literal and figurative, has played a central role in our collective and individual experiences. In many such trials, the Jews have stood in the dock—much as Abraham did in King Nimrod's court—accused of the widest and wildest array of crimes, ranging from deicide, to ritual murder, to poisoning of wells, to blasphemy, to false conversion, to treason. Sometimes the defendant has been an individual Jew, such as Jesus, Alfred Dreyfus, Mendel Beilis, or Leo Frank. Sometimes it is "the Jews" in general. Most recently, it has been the nation-state of the Jewish people.

It should not be surprising that Shakespeare's only play about a Jew, Shylock, would feature the trial of a Jewish moneylender by self-righteous Christians. Nor should it be surprising that modern political Zionism, as espoused by Theodor Herzl, should, at least according to tradition, grow out of a trial—the court-martial of Alfred Dreyfus.[1] Likewise, the Anti-Defamation League was created in response to the trial of Leo Frank.[2] Many of the central tragedies of Jewish history—the trial and crucifixion of Jesus, for which the Jews were blamed; the Inquisition; the martyrology of the great rabbis; the disputations between Christianity and Judaism; the blood libels; the earliest Nazi attacks against "enemies of the state"; the Stalinist purges; McCarthyism—involved trials, though "trials" whose outcomes were often predetermined.

In the twenty-first century, Israel and Zionism seem always to be on trial—at the United Nations, in international tribunals, on university campuses, and in the "court of public opinion." I have been privileged to be among the defense lawyers for the modern nation-state of the Jewish people.[3]

Perhaps as a result of always being on trial, the Jewish people have produced an extraordinary array of Jewish lawyers, some of whom have become defenders of accused Jews, while others have played major roles in the legal systems of their adopted countries and of the world.

In Part II of this book, I will discuss Jews on trial—first as defendants, then as defenders. I will first allude to several of the most transformative trials of Jews and explore the reasons why the Jewish people have so often stood in the dock of history, how history has prepared us to defend against false and malicious charges, and how we have handled our unsought status as defendants and pariahs.

I will then discuss Jewish defenders—lawyers who have followed in the footsteps of Abraham, the idol smasher, the advocate, the conciliator, the collaborator, the rescuer of prisoners, and the deal maker. Some such lawyers transcend categorization. Others fit neatly into one of the Abrahamic categories. In selecting lawyers for inclusion, I define the concept of the "Jewish lawyer" broadly to include anyone with a legal education and a Jewish heritage.[4] I include one honorary Jew and two honorary law-yers, for reasons that will become apparent. Most of the Jewish lawyers I discuss are deceased. Only a few remain active.

So let us now turn to some of these trials and explore the question of why Jews, who have played such a disproportionally positive role in developing and implementing the rule of law and the adversarial system of justice, have so often been victimized by injustice administered under the pretext of "justice" and with the false imprimatur of "law." As Justice Robert Jackson, who served as America's first chief prosecutor at the Nuremberg trials, once put it, "The most odious of all oppressions are those which mask as justice."[5] Throughout history, Jews have been victimized by the masks of justice hiding the grotesque faces of injustice. It has been the role of the Abrahamic defenders of justice to rip off these masks and expose the ugly truth.

# 5

---

# The Trial of Jesus, the Conviction of the Jews, and the Blood Libel

Although several biblical characters, including Abraham, were subjected to "trials," the trial that has had the most profound influence on Jewish history was that of Jesus of Nazareth, a young Jewish rabbi who challenged the authority of other rabbis and of the Roman Empire.

In addition to being a rabbi, Jesus was a talented "lawyer," employing legal logic to defeat older rabbis in disputations. The Christian Bible gives several examples of Jesus's lawyerly skills, such as when the Pharisees asked him whether an adulteress must be stoned according to Mosaic law. Jesus, the defense attorney, replied, "He that is without sin among you, let him cast the first stone." Or when Jesus was asked whether it is lawful to pay tribute to Caesar, and Jesus, the conciliator, replied, "Render unto Caesar the things that are Caesar's; and unto God the things that are God's."

The trial, conviction, and crucifixion of Jesus—and the subsequent "confession" and "conviction" of "all" the Jews and their "children" for this "deicide"—have had a transformative impact not only on Jewish history but on the subsequent trials of individual Jews that have been conducted under the shadow of the "deicide" and the "blood libel."

In my autobiography, I recount the following exchange I once had with Woody Allen about this issue:

[Woody] . . . asked me which dead person I would have wanted to represent as a criminal lawyer. I immediately replied, "Jesus."

"Do you think you could have won?" he asked.

"In front of a Jewish jury, maybe."

"Those biblical Jews were tough. They didn't tolerate trouble-makers like Jesus. They probably wouldn't have liked Jews like us from Brooklyn," Woody mused.

"Yeah, but imagine how different history would be if a Jewish lawyer saved Jesus. They couldn't accuse us of killing their Lord."

"But he wouldn't have been their Lord, if you had won. He wouldn't have been crucified. And without crucifixion, there's no Christianity, so if you had won they'd be blaming the Jews for destroying Christianity."

"But there wouldn't be any 'they' to blame us," I replied.

"There's always a 'they,' " Woody said, smiling.[1]

Only Jews could make a joke out of the two-millennium-long accusation that we are "Christ killers," guilty of deicide. Although the crucifixion of Jesus was ordered by the Roman governor, one Gospel placed the responsibility squarely on the Jews. According to Matthew 27, the governor, Pontius Pilate, "washed his hands" of the crime and shouted to the Jewish crowd, "I am innocent of this man's blood." The Jews—"all the people"—answered, "His blood is on us and on our children," thus giving rise to the first "blood libel," the claim that *all* the Jews throughout history were guilty of killing Jesus.[2]

Again, it took a Jewish comedian to expose the absurdity of this collective accusation. Lenny Bruce had a bit about his friend Morty, who was tired of all the Jews being blamed for killing Jesus, so he decided to take the rap himself:

Yes, we did it. I did it. My family. I found a note in my basement: "We killed him—signed, Morty."[3]

Later, when Lenny Bruce was accused of being a Christ killer, he replied, "It wasn't me. It was Morty. I have an alibi. I was at the movies."

But for many Jews throughout history, the charge of deicide was anything but a joke.

Pogroms would be directed against the "Christ killers," especially during the Easter season, which commemorated the crucifixion. Thousands, perhaps more, of Jews were murdered in revenge for this collective "crime." Others, like Mendel Beilis, were put on trial, as recently as 1913 in Kiev, for "the blood libel"—the historical accusation of Jewish ritual killing of a Christian child to use his blood for the baking of Passover matzoth.[4] A priest testified to the "truth" of the claim that the Jewish religion requires the ritual murder of Christian children and the use of their blood in Passover matzoth. Remarkably, Beilis was successfully defended by a Jewish lawyer and acquitted. He quickly immigrated to America. There were other blood libels after the Beilis trial, especially during the Nazi era in Europe and in parts of the Muslim world. Even today, the Jews of Ukraine are not entirely free from fear that they will be attacked as Christ killers.[5]

The "blood libel" might have originally derived from the fiction that Jews were required to reenact the crucifixion during Passover by shedding the blood of a Christian child. Several of the "martyred" children were officially sanctified by the Catholic and Russian Orthodox Churches, thus lending credibility to the blood libel.

Chaucer mentions the case of "Little Saint Hugh of Lincoln," an eight-year-old whose body was found in a well belonging to a Jew, who then "confessed" that the boy had been crucified by "the Jews."[6] Ninety Jews of Lincoln were then arrested and tried for the crime. Eighteen of them were executed.[7]

In my home, I have a printed blood libel proclamation from Nuremberg, dated 1490, accusing the Jews of martyring Simon of Trent, a two-year-old whose body was found on Easter Sunday in 1475. Twenty-three Jews were arrested and tortured over that episode. Nineteen were executed.[8]

Walter Laqueur has estimated that there have been about 150 recorded cases involving the blood libel, thousands of rumored accusations, and countless mob attacks and pogroms incited by this lie.[9]

Amazingly, some people still believe the blood libel to be true or at least arguable, including at least one widely published self-described "proud self-hating Jew" and former Israeli, Gilad Atzmon.[10] In his book

*The Wandering Who?*—which was praised by the likes of Professors Richard Falk and John Mearsheimer[11]—Atzmon, who has expressed doubts regarding the historical accuracy of the Holocaust, suggests that schoolchildren should question, as he does, "how the teacher could know that these accusations of Jews making *Matza* out of young Goyim's blood were indeed empty or groundless,"[12] thus suggesting that they may be true or at least subject to classroom discussion. (This from a hater who writes that "from [a] certain ideological perspective, Israel is actually far worse than Nazi Germany"[13]—a modern-day blood libel against the nation-state of the Jewish people.)

But except for a few nutcases and conspiracy theorists like Atzmon, the only groups that still push variations on this discredited libel are Islamic extremists, some of whom have produced films and television shows[14] that include the claim that Jews murder children for their blood.[15]

In May 2013, an Egyptian politician named Khaled Zaafrani related the following blood libel during a television interview:

> It is well-known that during Passover they make matzos called the "Blood of Zion." They take a Christian child, slit his throat and slaughter him . . . they never forgo this rite.[16]

During the Passover 2013 season, a Web site belonging to an organization started by Hanan Ashrawi of the Palestinian Authority condemned President Obama for hosting a Seder in the White House, asking the following rhetorical question: "Does Obama in fact know the relationship, for example, between 'Passover' and 'Christian blood'?! Or 'Passover' and 'Jewish blood rituals'?!" It then asserted that "much of the chatter and gossip about historical Jewish blood rituals in Europe are real and not fake as they claim; the Jews used the blood of Christians in the Jewish Passover."[17]

Today, for the most part, the blood libel is used in connection with other falsehoods directed at the Jewish people and its nation-state. This has been the case when the false charges have been directed against Jews, such as Alfred Dreyfus, Leo Frank, and various perceived enemies of the Soviet Union. Much has been written about these cases, and I will briefly recount them here only to illustrate the phenomenon of individual Jews being placed on trial as surrogates for the Jewish people. The Dreyfus trial near the turn of the twentieth century, which began as a conventional court-martial, quickly turned into a generalized defamation against the Jews of Europe, accusing them of disloyalty to their "adopted" countries.[18]

# 6

## Alfred Dreyfus, Leo Frank, Rudolf Slansky, Anatoly Sharansky, and the Nation-State of the Jewish People on Trial

The false charge of dual loyalty directed against Jews who live in "other people's" countries goes back to the Bible, where the Egyptians, the Persians, and other host nations worried that their Jewish neighbors could not be trusted to be singularly loyal to their adopted homelands. The Dreyfus case raised that specter in the context of a false charge of spying directed against an assimilated Jewish officer in the French army.[1]

The biblical prohibition against bearing false witness grows out of the story of Joseph's being framed by Potiphar's wife on a charge of attempted rape.[2] In our world, the frame-up of an innocent citizen by government officials is generally the stuff of novels and motion pictures. Sure, there are mistakes: some innocent defendants are wrongly convicted. Occasionally, there is a frame-up attempt by a private enemy or even by an individual policeman. But the government frame-up, orchestrated at the highest levels, is not a part of the American experience. Though some claim that frame-ups have occurred in our recent past—in the Sacco and Vanzetti, Rosenberg, and Peltier cases,[3] to mention some of the most notorious—the evidence in support of such a hypothesis is, at best, inconclusive.

# Alfred Dreyfus

There is no remaining doubt, however, that Alfred Dreyfus was, in fact, framed for a crime committed by someone else. The "Dreyfus affair," as it has come to be known, is a sordid tale of judicial corruption at the highest levels. It could not have been accomplished without the active complicity of the military, the prosecution, the judiciary, and others within the government. Nor could injustice have prevailed for so long without the acquiescence of the mainstream press, high officials of the Catholic Church, many intellectuals and artists, and large elements of the populace.

Eventually, the fraud was exposed by a handful of courageous journalists, lawyers, and relatives of the accused. France was transformed, first by Dreyfus's wrongful conviction and later by his vindication.

In the beginning, the evidence of Dreyfus's guilt seemed absolutely overwhelming. Indeed, it *was* overwhelming. It also happened to be false, though not obviously so. The evidence consisted largely of handwritten documents. The first was written by an unnamed French officer spying for the Germans. The handwriting bore some resemblance to Dreyfus's, and thus suspicion was focused on the Alsatian Jew. The fact that Dreyfus was Jewish made him the perfect suspect at a time of rampant anti-Semitism, especially in the French military and among elements in the Catholic Church. Organized anti-Semites (who had their own newspapers, societies, and parties) used the accusation against Dreyfus as a rallying point. He was convicted by the General Staff of the military and in the press even before his court-martial. Though the evidence was speculative at best, the honor of the military was at stake. Accordingly, a secret file, which was far more persuasive than the public file, was assembled and clandestinely turned over to the court-martial to assuage any doubts about the handwriting. The secret file included a smoking gun—a document specifically referring to Dreyfus. But unbeknownst to the court-martial, that document was a not-so-clever forgery. It was clever enough, however, in the absence of challenge from the defense, which had no idea the file even existed, to persuade the court-marital to convict.

Dreyfus was sentenced to Devil's Island, a hellhole from which few returned. A devoted brother, a few skeptical journalists, some brave politicians, and a handful of honest military men kept the case alive, even as its victim barely survived the rigors of deportation. Slowly, the prosecution's case began to crumble. First it was discovered that another officer's handwriting bore a closer resemblance to the original incriminating document than Dreyfus's. Then it was proved that the smoking-gun document was a forgery. But there was no relief for Dreyfus. Émile Zola came to Dreyfus's defense with his famous "J'accuse."[4] Still there was no relief. Indeed, Zola himself was sentenced to a year in jail for publishing his essay.

Eventually, Dreyfus was granted a new trial. He was again convicted, this time over the dissent of two judges. He was pardoned but not vindicated. Finally, public opinion was reversed, and Dreyfus was exonerated, officially declared innocent, and restored to his rank in the army. Careers were made and broken over the Dreyfus affair, and the course of history was changed, not only in France, but also throughout the world.

In France, the Dreyfus case marked the decline of the influence of both the military and the church. It signaled the beginning of distrust in conservative institutions, such as the judiciary and bureaucracy.

For Jews throughout the world, the Dreyfus case and its accompanying anti-Semitic hysteria also constituted a turning point. The seeds of Hitler's Holocaust could be sensed in the cries for a "massacre" of all the Jewish "synagogue lice" and shouts of "Death to the Jews."[5] A military physician proposed "vivisection of Jews rather than harmless rabbits," and there were calls for "all the kikes and kikettes and their kiddy-kikes [to be] placed in glass furnaces."[6] A young Viennese journalist covering the Dreyfus affair was stimulated to write a book called *The Jewish State*.[7] His name was Theodor Herzl, and his idea became known as political Zionism, which led to the establishment of Israel some fifty years later.

The greatest impact of the Dreyfus affair was on the law, both in France and throughout the world. The name Dreyfus became synonymous with governmental frame-up. The case became a rallying cry for increased judicial protection for criminal defendants. The frame-up became a real possibility to be protected against by fair procedures. Dreyfus's false conviction became to European justice what Joseph's false conviction had been to the biblical admonition against bearing false witness.

But parchment admonitions are not enough. The Dreyfus case reminded the world of how fragile our liberty is, how easy it is to lose it in the name of governmental power, and how essential it is to protect it by fail-safe procedures. Unfortunately, we need no reminder that anti-Semitism, perhaps in different guises, is still rampant among a significant portion of the French and other European populations. The grandchildren of Frenchmen who called for the massacre of the Jews during the Dreyfus trial helped to round up the Jews of Vichy, France. And now some of their grandchildren are singling out the nation-state of the Jewish people for divestment, boycotts, and sanctions.

In the United States, anti-Semitism is largely a thing of the past, but shortly after the Dreyfus case it was still prevalent in parts of our nation, as became evident during the trial of Leo Frank and its tragic aftermath.

## Leo Frank

The trial, conviction, death sentence, and eventual lynching of Leo Frank during the second decade of the twentieth century constitute a major episode not only in Jewish and American history but also in the development of American political and legal institutions.[8] It was the only instance of an American Jew's being lynched, and it generated, or revealed, an enormous amount of anti-Semitism in the Deep South. The Knights of Mary Phagan, formed to avenge the murder of the young factory worker for which Frank was convicted, became an important component of the twentieth-century resurrection of the Ku Klux Klan.[9] The Anti-Defamation League of B'nai B'rith was founded in reaction to the anti-Semitism generated—or at least disclosed—by the Frank case.[10]

Sometimes characterized as the "American Dreyfus case," the trial and appeals of Leo Frank in Atlanta, Georgia, were conducted in a carnival atmosphere. Crowds—mobs, really—sang "The Ballad of Mary Phagan," which included the following lyrics:

Little Mary Phagan . . .

She left her home at eleven,
She kissed her mother good-by;
Not one time did the poor child think
That she was a-going to die.

Leo Frank he met her
With a brutish heart, we know;
He smiled, and said, "Little Mary,
You won't go home no more."

Sneaked along behind her
Till she reached the metal-room;
He laughed, and said, "Little Mary,
You have met your fatal doom."

Down upon her knees
To Leo Frank she plead;
He taken a stick from the trash-pile
And struck her across the head.[11]

Crowds inside the courtroom shouted anti-Jewish epithets and demanded Frank's death. The smell of the lynch mob was in the air.

The state's star witness was James Conley, a black maintenance worker at the factory that Frank managed and at which Mary Phagan worked. Conley testified that Frank killed the young girl, ordered him to dispose of the body, and then dictated notes that placed the blame on a "Negro."

When the jury convicted Frank, it was the first time in memory that a white man had been convicted of murder on the basis of the uncorroborated testimony of a black witness. This apparent advance in racial justice was explained away by a local observer who said, "That wasn't a white man convicted by that N———'s testimony. It was a Jew."

One of the members of Frank's defense team was the prominent Jewish lawyer Louis Marshall, who helped prepare a petition to the Supreme Court.[12] Marshall was a human rights lawyer who was among the founders of the National Association for the Advancement of Colored People (NAACP). He is reported to have argued more cases in the Supreme Court than any lawyer of his time.[13] But he was not successful in the Frank case, and Leo Frank's fate was in the hands of the governor, who decided to commute Frank's death sentence and leave him to serve out a term of life imprisonment. That appeared to be a great victory for Frank and his many supporters around the country, because the evidentiary foundation underlying Frank's conviction was beginning to crumble as a result of the discovery of new evidence strongly suggesting that it was the government's star witness—not Frank—who had killed the victim. It seemed only a matter of time before Frank would be freed from his imprisonment.

In order to prevent Frank's freedom, several of the "best" citizens of Georgia—including a minister, a former governor, two former Georgia Supreme Court justices, the son of a former senator, an ex-sheriff, and a sitting judge—decided to take the law into their own hands.

They constituted themselves as a vigilante committee and let it be known that they intended to kidnap Frank from prison and lynch him. Despite some perfunctory efforts by prison authorities to protect their controversial prisoner, the lynch mob had little difficulty entering the prison and kidnapping Frank without firing a shot. It was obvious that at least some of the prison authorities were in on the plan. Frank was taken to Marietta, where he was lynched and his body desecrated.

The residents of Marietta knew exactly who was involved in the lynching; indeed, some members of the lynch mob boasted about their participation and gave interviews to the press. Photographs of the lynching and souvenir pieces of the rope were sold throughout Georgia. Nonetheless, the grand jury investigating the murder of Leo Frank—which included at least "seven members of the Lynch Party"[14]—concluded that it was unable to identify any of the perpetrators. This was typical of lynchings in the South during that era. The only difference was that this victim was not black.[15]

Nearly seventy years after Leo Frank's murder, new evidence of his innocence emerged. An eighty-two-year-old man, who had been a youthful eyewitness to events surrounding the killing of Mary Phagan, finally came forward and told what he had seen back in 1913. His evidence contradicted the state's star witness and strongly suggested that the murder was committed by that same witness, the black maintenance man.[16] The murderer threatened the young witness with death if he ever mentioned what he had observed, and he did not come forward for all those years. Now he has told his story, and it seems to have persuaded most objective people that Leo Frank was lynched for a crime committed by someone else.

Finally, in 1986, Frank was posthumously pardoned with the following official apology:

> The lynching aborted the legal process, thus foreclosing further effort to prove Frank's [i]nnocence. It resulted from the State of Georgia's failure to protect Frank. Compounding the injustice, the State then failed to prosecute any of the lynchers.[17]

Remarkably, some Georgians continued to resist this pardon. For Leo Frank, the apology came too late, as did another apology, when the Soviet Union rehabilitated the many Jews it murdered during Stalin's reign of terror.

## Rudolf Slansky

Jews have had a complex relationship with the extreme Left in general and with Soviet Communism in particular. Jews were among the leaders of the Bolshevik Revolution. They were also among its victims. In

1952, the Jewish leadership of the Communist Party of Czechoslovakia was put on trial and charged with an "anti-state conspiracy."[18] In reality, it was the culmination of a long-term Stalinist campaign to purge Jews from the leadership of the party. Rudolf Slansky[19] and eleven other Jews were accused of being part of a "Trotskyite-Zionist conspiracy," despite the reality that Trotsky was an anti-Zionist. (I'm reminded of the story of a Communist demonstration at City College in New York where the police were beating up Communist demonstrators. One student pleaded, "Stop hitting me, I'm an anti-Communist." The cop responded, "I don't care what kind of Communist you are," and continued to beat him.)

Slansky and the others were tortured into making false confessions and then executed. In reporting on this trial, *The New York Times* observed,

> If this were only a rehash of the [Stalinist show trials] of the Nineteen Thirties, we might regard [it] as purely a Soviet farce playing a return run in a new adaptation. But there is something new in this latest trial. This is the charge that Slansky and the majority of his fellow-defendants who are of Jewish origin were members of a vast Zionist conspiracy, betraying their country to "American imperialism" in order to serve the state of Israel. . . . Here we have the infamous Protocols of the Elders of Zion again, but in a Stalinist version. . . .
>
> So the Prague trial is not entirely a comedy; rather it may well mark the beginning of major tragedy as the Kremlin swings further and further toward anti-Semitism masked as anti-Zionism.[20]

The Slansky trial became the basis of the award-winning French-Italian film *The Confession*, by Costa-Gavras, starring Yves Montand and Simone Signoret.

The Slansky trial was not the only anti-Jewish prosecution directed against prominent political, artistic, or otherwise visible Jews. Before, during, and after World War II, hundreds of prominent Russian Jews—artists, musicians, writers, and political leaders—were "tried," convicted, and murdered.[21] This reign of terror continued until Stalin's sudden death in 1953, which was initially attributed to a plot by his Jewish doctors—a Communist variation on the blood libel. This accusation was part of the more general "doctors' plot," in which a group of prominent Jewish doctors were charged with a conspiracy to murder leaders of the Communist Party.[22] The so-called trial of the Jewish doctors was actually under way when Stalin died. It was supposed to be a prelude to the mass deportation of Soviet Jews to the east.

It is remarkable, but perhaps not surprising, that within less than a decade from the end of the Holocaust, the Soviet Union—which fought Hitler and liberated many of the death camps—would blame the Jews for all its problems and plan the deportation of the Jews of Moscow, Leningrad, and other large cities to Birobidjan. Each of these deportation plans might have grown out of the anti-Semitic paranoia of one man, Stalin. But Stalin alone could not have carried out his devious plan, any more than Hitler alone could have carried out the plan he adumbrated in *Mein Kampf.* A deep-seated anti-Semitism was pervasive both in the Soviet Union and in Germany, as well as in many other European countries.[23]

To be sure, this plan was not carried out after Stalin's death in 1953—a death that might have been prevented or at least delayed had Stalin not had his Jewish doctors arrested.


## Anatoly Sharansky

There were few subsequent trials of Jews—as Jews—until the 1970s, when many of the leaders of the Jewish refusenik and dissident movement were placed on trial. I was one of the lawyers who represented these defendants. The trials were a mockery. When I first traveled to the Soviet Union in 1974 as part of a legal defense team headed by a great non-Jewish lawyer, Telford Taylor, I was advised by my clients not to expect justice. One of them told me the story of the Czech minister who visited the Kremlin to ask for financial assistance to set up a department of the navy in Prague. His Soviet counterpart mocked him, asking rhetorically, "Why do you need a department of the navy? You're a landlocked country without a navy"—to which the Czech replied, "But you have a department of justice!"

The most prominent of these trials, and the one covered most widely in the world media, was the "treason" trial of Anatoly Sharansky. He was arrested in 1977 and initially charged with spying for the United States, which carried a death penalty. His wife and his mother asked Irwin Cotler and me to represent him, but we were not allowed to attend his trial. I went to the White House and requested of President Carter that he announce that Sharansky had never spied for the United States. Carter did so, and that capital charge was dropped. But Sharansky was convicted of other charges and sentenced to a long prison term in the Gulag. In his closing statement to the court, Sharansky, knowing his fate was sealed, boldly told the court, "I say to my wife and to my people, *Leshana haba'a b'Yerushalayim* [Next year in Jerusalem]. . . . And to the court, which has only to read a sentence that was prepared long ago—to you I have nothing to say."[24] It took more than "next year," but eventually we worked out a multiparty prisoner exchange that resulted in Sharansky's release, and he immediately made aliya to Israel.

In all these Soviet Union cases, we prepared briefs *as if* justice mattered, and in the end we helped to release numerous prisoners and assisted numerous refuseniks in immigrating to Israel and the United States. Our briefs alone would never, of course, have been taken seriously, but in combination with economic, political, and diplomatic pressure they provided a legal basis for the Soviets to act as they did. We might not have gotten justice, but we did get results.


## The Nation-State of the Jewish People on Trial

The current manifestation of "Jews on trial" involves not individual Jews[25] but the nation-state of the Jewish people, despite the reality that Israel's "birth certificate" has more legal, political, and moral validity than that of almost any other nation. The nation-state of the Jewish people was established with the approval of the United Nations and the prior approval of the League of Nations. It was born of law, not revolution or conquest, as were so many other countries. Much of the land that became the heart of Israel was purchased, as Abraham's was, for a fair price, and from distant landlords. As soon as Israel declared statehood in 1948, it was recognized by the United States, the Soviet Union, the European countries, and most of the rest of the world. Then it was attacked by surrounding countries and lost 1 percent of its population in defending its statehood and its people.

Yet since that time, its very existence has been "on trial" in international forums and in the court of public opinion. In 1975, the General Assembly of the United Nations placed Zionism—the national liberation movement of the Jewish people—on trial. After a series of speeches by enemies of the nation-state of the Jewish people, the General Assembly adopted the most infamous resolution in its history, resolution 3379, declaring that "Zionism is a form of racism and racial discrimination." Seventy-two countries voted in favor, including, ironically, Cambodia, which was then in the process of murdering millions of its own citizens without any expression of concern from the United Nations. Thirty-five nations voted against, and thirty-two abstained. This and other similar actions by the General Assembly led Abba Eban to proclaim that "if Algeria introduced a resolution declaring that the earth was flat and that Israel had flattened it, it would pass by a vote of 164 to 13 with 26 abstentions."[26] Addressing the assembly, the U.S. representative to the United Nations, Daniel Patrick Moynihan, fumed that "the United States rises to declare before the General Assembly of the United Nations and before the world that it does not acknowledge, it will not abide by, it will never acquiesce in this infamous act."[27]

The result of this resolution was that "Zionists" were blacklisted and banned from speaking at several colleges and universities that had "anti-racist" speaking policies. In a world where genocide, slavery, disappearances, torture, systematic rape, murder of dissidents, and other grave violations of human rights were being routinely perpetrated by its member nations, Zionism and Israel became the number one enemy of the UN, with more resolutions condemning Israel than all the other member nations combined. The judge and jury were stacked against Israel as it was repeatedly placed in the dock.

The Zionism-equals-racism resolution was ultimately rescinded in 1991 by a vote of the General Assembly,[28] but it continued to animate UN actions, especially by the Human Rights Council of the UN (previously known as the UN Commission on Human Rights). In 2001, it convened the first of several Durban Conferences against "racism, racial discrimination, xenophobia and related intolerance." Its primary focus was on Israel, which again stood alone in the dock. The Durban Conference ignored racial genocides, slavery, and other obvious manifestations of racism and discrimination. The final preparatory session was held in Tehran. Israeli and Jewish NGOs were excluded.

According to Professor Irwin Cotler, who attended the conference, the air was filled with hate speech, with people expressing sentiments such as "Too bad that the Holocaust was not completed."[29] The conference became a "festival of hate such that we had not experienced anywhere at any time before."[30] To Cotler, it was "the most dangerous form of antisemitism that we are witnessing in the twenty-first century."[31] And all of this was done under the aegis of the UN.

The late California congressman Tom Lantos, a Holocaust survivor, observed,

> Whenever the word "Holocaust" was read during the plenary review of the combined text, one of the Islamic delegates—usually Egypt—intervened to change "Holocaust" to "holocausts." Adding insult to injury, the same delegates requested that the phrase "and the ethnic cleansing of the Arab population in historic Palestine" be inserted after the appearance of "holocausts."[32]

A second Durban Conference was held in Geneva in 2009. Although the United States, Canada, Italy, and several other countries boycotted what had by this time become clear would be another hate conference, I decided to travel to Geneva in an effort to restore the human rights agenda to its proper priorities or, if that wasn't possible, to expose the UN Human Rights Council for what it had become—an enemy of neutral and universal human rights. It would be an uphill fight because the primary speaker invited to address the second Durban Conference was Mahmoud Ahmadinejad, the Holocaust-denying then president of Iran.

I worked with several genuine human rights organizations in an effort to shame the Human Rights Council into broadening its agenda to include the genocides in Africa and other serious human rights abuses around the globe. We brought real victims of human rights abuses from Rwanda, Darfur, and other locations where genocides had been ignored by the UN. We conducted a parallel human rights conference in which we took testimony from these victims and witnesses, to whom the UN had refused to listen. I also delivered an address on the inversion of "human rights" and "human wrongs."

I was staying in the same hotel as Ahmadinejad. My wife and I were having a drink in the lobby bar when Ahmadinejad and his entourage paraded through the lobby. He looked at us and smiled. I approached one of his handlers, introduced myself, and told him that I challenge the president to a debate about the Holocaust. He asked, "Where, at Harvard?" Ahmadinejad had previously spoken at Columbia University, and I suspected that he might welcome an invitation from Harvard. I replied, "No, the debate should be at Auschwitz; that's where the evidence is." He said he would communicate my offer to the president, who, he told me, was on the way to a press conference. I went and tried to ask Ahmadinejad whether he would debate me at Auschwitz. I was immediately hauled off by the Swiss police, removed from the hotel, and told I would not be allowed to return "for security reasons." I insisted that "security reasons" did not justify protecting the president from a hostile question. They told me that my belongings would be removed from my room and my key changed. I immediately called someone I knew in the Obama administration, who phoned the U.S. consulate in Geneva, and I was allowed back in the hotel with an apology. The photograph of my being forcibly removed from the hotel was flashed around the world, with the following caption:

> Harvard Law professor Alan Dershowitz is led away after declaring he planned to challenge Iranian President Mahmoud Ahmadinejad about his views on the Holocaust and Israel minutes before the meeting between Swiss President Hans-Rudolf Merz and the Iranian president in Geneva, Switzerland, on April 19, 2009.

The next day Ahmadinejad was scheduled to give his address. We were not allowed into the chamber but were told to go to a special room where we could watch and listen to his talk. We assembled and watched as Ahmadinejad was greeted with applause by many of the delegates. When he began to speak, we discovered that his words, delivered in Farsi, were not being translated to our room, but only to the assembly chamber. So I led a march into the assembly chamber. Several delegations were absent, and we took their seats. As soon as Ahmadinejad denied the Holocaust, which he did near the beginning of his speech, I stood up and shouted "Shame!" and walked out, passing directly in front of his lectern. Many others walked out as well, including several European delegations. Ahmadinejad's talk was a fiasco and was so reported by the media. He had made a fool of himself—with our help.

The following year, the Durban Conference on human rights was convened in New York. Once again, we convened parallel conferences. In my address, I made the following point:

> One important reason why there is no peace in the Middle East can be summarized tragically in two letters: UN. That building, dedicated in theory to peace, has facilitated terrorism, stood idly by genocide, given a platform to Holocaust deniers, and disincentivized the Palestinians from negotiating a reasonable two-state solution. . . .

How dare states such as Saudi Arabia, Cuba, Venezuela, Zimbabwe, Iran, Bahrain, Syria, Belarus, and other tyrannies too numerous to mention . . . lecture Israel about human rights? How dare states such as Turkey, that have attacked their own Kurdish minorities and Armenian minorities, and Russia, which has attacked its own Chechnyan minority, . . . lecture Israel about peace?

Is there no sense of shame . . . ? Has the word "hypocrisy" lost all meaning . . . ? Does no one recognize the need for a single, neutral standard of human rights? Have human rights now become the permanent weapon of choice for those who practice human wrongs? For shame. For shame.[33]

The latest form of "trial" faced by Israel is the movement to single out the nation-state of the Jewish people for boycott, divestment, and sanctions (BDS).[34] Israel has been placed on trial before many university senates and other student and faculty bodies.[35]

Even if the BDS movement is defeated, Israel will remain on trial, not so much for what it does as for what it is—the democratic nation-state of the Jewish people, while living amid undemocratic theocracies, tyrannies, and failed states. There are also efforts under way to bring charges against Israeli political and military leaders in front of the International Criminal Court, despite Israel's efforts to reduce civilian casualties in the face of human shields being employed by Hamas and other terrorist groups.[36] In the end—like those falsely accused of the blood libel and other made-up "crimes"—Israel will be vindicated by the verdict of history, but only after paying a heavy price.

## Why the Jews?

Why have so many Jews been placed on trial throughout the millennia, convicted, often executed, and then vindicated by the judgment of history? This query is a variation on the old question "Why the

Jews?" The shortest poem in history goes as follows: "How odd of God / To choose the Jews."[37] How odd of prosecutors and persecutors to choose the Jews. Why?

There's an old expression in Poland that goes something like this: "If something has gone wrong, the Jews must be involved." From the killing of Jesus to the spread of the Black Plague to the poisoning of wells to the killing of Christian children, to the Bolshevik Revolution to the drug trade, to inflation, to depression—all these have been blamed on the Jews.

Karl Marx, who was born to a Jewish family, identified the evils of capitalism with "the Jews," whereas Edmund Burke identified the evils of radicalism with "the Jews."[38] Throughout history, both the hard Left and the hard Right have blamed "the Jews" for the problems of the world. If there are problems, it must be the fault of the Jews. Accordingly, if any group is to be placed in the dock of history and tried for crimes against humanity, it follows logically and empirically, according to this perverse worldview, that it must be "the Jews"—not necessarily individuals who happen to be Jews (though this too has been common), but "the Jews" as a group. So the poorest shtetl-dwelling peasant is as guilty of the crimes of capitalist exploitation as a Rothschild, according to Marx, and the Rothschilds are as guilty of revolutionary crimes as the Jew on the barricades, according to Burke.[39] Their real crime is not what they have *done* but rather what they are—namely, Jews.

These "imaginary Jews," as one writer has called them, have been the scapegoats of the Western world for millennia. Now, with globalization and the United Nations, they have become scapegoats for much of the rest of the world. This "blame the Jews" mentality has provided "one of the most powerful theoretical systems 'for making sense of [a] world'" that often defies logical understanding.[40]

Recently, a British parliamentarian named Clare Short said that Israel might cause the end of the human race because it diverts the world's attention from the problem of global warming.[41] And a Honduran cardinal—who had been on the short list for pope—blamed the pedophile scandal within the Catholic Church on Israel and the Jews.[42]

Just read Article 22 of the current Hamas charter for a catalog of Jewish sins:

> The enemies have been scheming for a long time . . . and have accumulated huge and influential material wealth. With their money, they took control of the world media. . . . With their money they stirred revolutions in various parts of the globe. . . . They stood behind the French Revolution, the Communist Revolution and most of the revolutions we hear about. . . . With their money they formed secret organizations—such as the Freemasons, Rotary Clubs and the Lions—which are spreading around the world, in order to destroy societies and carry out Zionist interests. . . . They stood behind World War I . . . and formed the League of Nations through which they could rule the world. They were behind World War II, through which they made huge financial gains. . . . There is no war going on anywhere without them having their finger in it.[43]

This contemporary variation on the infamous forgery the *Protocols of the Elders of Zion* is common fare in Islamic and Arab media. Other variations are increasingly visible in Hungary, Greece, Lithuania, and other European countries. They are widely circulated on the Internet.[44]

It should not be surprising therefore that Jews—individually, as a people, and as a nation—have been put on trial. What is deeply surprising is how pervasive it is even today. Just search the Web and you will find the Jews or their nation-state blamed for every current catastrophe from the tsunami in the Pacific, to 9/11, to the problems of Ukraine.[45] It actually made news when neither Israel nor Jews were blamed for Malaysia Airlines Flight 370.[46]

Just as blacks could not justly be blamed for being lynched in the South, so too Jews and their state cannot be faulted for being placed in front of kangaroo courts. The finger must be pointed not at the falsely accused but at the false accusers. That is what Jewish lawyers who have defended the Jewish people and others against injustice have done over time. It is to that subject that we now turn.

# 7

## The Jewish Lawyer as Abrahamic Idol Smasher, Advocate, Collaborator, Rescuer, and Deal Maker

The first thing we do, let's kill all the lawyers." This directive, issued by the Shakespearean character Dick the Butcher,[1] has been the hallmark of tyrannical regimes. Hitler, Stalin, Mao, Khomeini, and other dictators did, in fact, start by killing lawyers, because lawyers are often at the forefront of challenging tyranny (at least those lawyers who aren't collaborating with it).

Among those who have been at the forefront of efforts to shatter the idols of Fascism, Communism, czarism, apartheid, segregation, and other evils have been lawyers, often Jewish lawyers. (They have also been at the forefront of efforts to dismantle capitalism, Fascism, Communism, and even Zionism—every ism but Darwinism!)[2] Wherever there have been idols, there have been Jewish lawyers smashing them and being smashed back by the idols and those who worship them. Abraham must be proud.

Tyrants always kill the most dangerous first, and lawyers have always been among the most dangerous revolutionaries, counterrevolutionaries, dissidents, and troublemakers. The immense catalog of such idol-smashing lawyers includes radicals who took leading roles in the American, French, Russian, Cuban, and other revolutions as well as in the sometimes-violent struggles against European colonialism, South African apartheid, and American segregation and in favor of freedom and self-determination, including the right of the Jewish people to a nation-state.[3]

In smashing idols, many Jewish lawyers—like Abraham—disrespected their parents and the religious traditions that were so central to their lives. Often they rejected their given names and adopted new names more suited to their revolutionary aspirations.[4] These idol smashers also left home, sometimes fearful of arrest, other times eager to export their new ideology and widen its impact. Like Abraham, some blamed the shattered idols on others, most particularly those in power. And like Abraham, some were willing to sacrifice their children and other family members to their new god. Again like the patriarch, many were placed on trial, some winning acquittals, others condemned to death.

In the coming pages, I will survey three categories of idol-smashing Jewish lawyers: Communist and other violent and hard-Left radicals; anti-Communist Soviet refuseniks and dissidents; and early Zionists, including some who advocated and/or engaged in violence. In subsequent pages, I will focus on Jewish lawyers who, in the spirit of the Abraham of the Sodom story, displayed chutzpah by arguing, respectfully but forcefully, with the authority figures of the day in the interest of fairness, due process, and human rights. I will then move to Jewish lawyers who, in the spirit of the Abraham of the Akedah, submitted to the immoral demands of those in power. Then I will discuss lawyers who, like Abraham rescuing Lot, have helped to redeem the imprisoned and persecuted. Finally, I will look at the role of the many traditional lawyers—deal makers, negotiators, commercial lawyers—who have made a difference in the world by doing well and doing good.

Although I focus only on a few handfuls of lawyers, each of them is an archetype representing many others too numerous to mention.

But before we turn to the impact Jewish lawyers have had on the world, we must define our terms. What exactly makes one a Jewish lawyer? Not surprisingly, there is even a dispute among Jewish law professors over exactly who qualifies as a Jewish lawyer. In a provocative essay in the *Cardozo Law Review* titled "Identifying the Jewish Lawyer," Professor Sanford Levinson of the University of Texas Law School points out the difficulty of defining who is a Jewish lawyer when we can't even agree on who is a Jew or who is a lawyer.[5]

Is "Jonathan Goldberg"—whose father is Jewish but whose mother is not and who never attends religious services but who considers himself Jewish—a Jew? Is that same "Jonathan Goldberg"—who graduated from law school, passed the bar, but now works as an investment banker—even a lawyer?

Levinson proposes an inclusive definition of "Jewish lawyer," while other Jewish law professors propose more specific, religiously based definitions. I am pleased to have been explicitly included in all the proposed definitions.

In one respect, of course, anyone named Dershowitz or Goldberg who graduated from law school is a Jewish lawyer.

For purposes of the forthcoming discussion, I define Jewish lawyer in the broadest and most inclusive terms.[6]

## Jewish Communist and Hard-Left Lawyers

Jews, including some lawyers, were instrumental in the Bolshevik Revolution, which overthrew the anti-Semitic czar, whose regime had relegated Jews to the Pale of Settlement and excluded them from educational and occupational opportunities. Other Jews—in the United States and Europe—became Communists during the 1930s when Communism was seen as the only ideology capable of defeating Fascism. Among the early Communist Jewish idol shatterers were Rosa Luxemburg and Emma Goldman. While only Luxemburg had a law degree, both of them had large followings among hard-Left Jewish lawyers. Luxemburg famously said, "I have no room in my heart for Jewish suffering." Ruth Fischer, a German Communist of Jewish background and a protégée of Luxemburg's, called on Germans to "shoot down the Jew-capitalist[s]; hang them from the lampposts."[7] Some Jewish Communists who did feel sympathy for fellow Jews left following the short-lived Hitler-Stalin pact and then returned when the Red Army defeated the Third Reich and liberated the death camps. Even after Stalin turned against Jewish artists, intellectuals, and "cosmopolitans"—murdering scores of them—some Jewish Communists retained their zeal for the Soviet Union, but most in the United States left the party before or during the period of McCarthyism that ended in the mid-1950s.

The story was different in South Africa, where the Communist Party was at the forefront of the struggle against apartheid. And at the forefront of the South African Communist Party were Jews, especially Jewish lawyers. They joined hands with Nelson Mandela and the African National Congress. Indeed, all five of the white defendants who stood in the dock along with Mandela at the Rivonia trial were Jews (and three of them were lawyers). So were several of the defense lawyers. A recent article titled "Mandela's Jewish Comrades" disclosed that

> the head count of white opponents of apartheid reads like a census list from one of the old shtetls in Lithuania (from where most South African Jews originated): Joe Slovo, Harold Wolpe, Ruth First, Albie Sachs, Ronald Segal, Dennis Goldberg, Rusty Bernstein, Solly Sachs, Helen Suzman, Ray Alexander, Ronnie Kasrils, Raymond Suttner, Ray Simons, Wolfie Kodish and many others. Some, like Ruth First, paid with their lives. Others were permanently disabled (Albie Sachs) or spent years in jail.[8]

Many of these Jewish idol smashers were lawyers, some of whom went underground, while others defended their more radical colleagues in the courtroom.

Most Jewish idol-smashing lawyers—especially the most radical—either gave up their identity as Jews or marginalized it in the interest of a "higher" calling, but some cited their Jewish heritage in support of their revolutionary zeal. Others, like Karl Marx—who studied law but abandoned it and who was a descendant of rabbis—became overt anti-Semites, radical atheists, or rabid anti-Zionists.

## Anti-Communist Idol Shatterers

Jews, and especially Jewish lawyers, have tended to be represented on both sides of many extreme movements. The radical Left has always had its share of Jewish lawyers, despite the hard Left's historical antagonism toward Jewish values and now toward the nation-state of the Jewish people. The conservative Right, with the obvious exception of Nazism, has also been supported by some Jews and Jewish lawyers. For example, the Federalist Society, a prominent conservative legal group, has many Jewish members. Free market economy supporters have always included Jewish lawyers. And remarkably, even Mussolini's early Fascism had some support among Italian Jews, including lawyers, though most Jews opposed Fascism and many of the most prominent leaders of the anti-Fascist movement were Italian Jews.[9]

Jews have also been among the leaders of anti-Communist movements, though few anti-Bolsheviks survived following the ascension to power of Lenin and Stalin, who had "enemies" of the state murdered, some after a "trial," others without even a semblance of legality.

It is against this background that the courage of the Jewish refusenik and dissident movement of the 1970s and 1980s must be viewed. These heroic idol shatterers challenged the authority of the powerful Soviet Union and the legitimacy of the Communist Party. The Jewish movement arose alongside the general democratic movement led by Andrei Sakharov, his Jewish wife, Elena Bonner, and others, some Jewish, some not. A few were lawyers; most were not.

Following the Six-Day War in 1967 and the publication of Elie Wiesel's eye-opening account of Soviet Jewry, *The Jews of Silence*, in 1966, many Jews in the Soviet Union began to rediscover or reassert their religious and cultural identity. Under Stalin, and even under his successors, Jews paid a heavy price for being openly Jewish. Moreover, Jewish institutions—synagogues, schools, and cultural events—were closed down or closely monitored.

Much has been written about the Jewish refusenik and dissident movement, including by me.[10] I coauthored a book with Telford Taylor called *Courts of Terror*, which contains the briefs we filed on behalf of several prisoners of conscience. It is enough here to note the remarkable courage of the Soviet Jews who stood up to repression, discrimination, violence, and lawlessness. They were the real heroes. They helped to shatter the false idol of totalitarian Communism. They helped to shatter the Iron Curtain and the Berlin Wall. They also showed how important it was— and still is—for the Jewish people to have a nation-state whose doors will always be open to refuseniks and dissidents. That was among the dreams of Zionism, based, as it was, on the nightmares of how Jews were treated in so many parts of the world.

## Zionist Idol Shatterers

It is quite remarkable that so many of the founders of Zionism and of the nation-state of the Jewish people were educated to be lawyers. These included Theodor Herzl, Ze'ev Jabotinsky, David Ben-Gurion, Menachem Begin, and Yitzhak Shamir. (Bruno Kreisky, the Jewish anti-Zionist chancellor of Austria, used to refer derisively to Prime Minister Begin as "that little Polish lawyer from Warsaw, or whatever he was.") None of them practiced law for any length of time, but several became idol smashers in the spirit of the young Abraham. Others became forceful advocates, arguing with authority on behalf of the Jewish people. All eventually became rescuers of the oppressed and purchasers of land when the nation of Israel was established as a place of asylum for persecuted Jews throughout the world.

The establishment of Israel required both legal advocacy and civil disobedience. Herzl and Ben-Gurion, aided by the nonlawyer Chaim Weizmann (he was a chemist), took the legal route of Abrahamic advocacy that ultimately led to the Balfour Declaration, the League of Nations' approval, and the United Nations' vote partitioning Palestine into two nation-states, for its Jewish and Arab inhabitants. Jabotinsky, Begin, and Shamir took the route of civil disobedience and of shattering idols that led to Great Britain's decision to end its mandate over Palestine and to leave that troubled land to its warring inhabitants.

The line between lawful advocacy and unlawful disobedience was never sharp. Ben-Gurion and Weizmann certainly condoned at least some civil disobedience while condemning terrorism. Jabotinsky, Begin, and Shamir supported legal actions while being convinced that such actions alone would never suffice. Both groups followed in the footsteps of Abraham, and both had as their goal the fulfillment of God's promise to Abraham with regard to the land of Israel.

It should not be surprising, therefore, that Israel was founded on the basis of legal enactments—the Balfour Declaration, resolutions of the League of Nations, a division of land ordained by the United Nations, and a formal declaration of independence by the new nation. Nor should it be surprising that Israel is a nation that operates under the rule of law, with a supreme court that is second to none in the world in enforcing legal standards against its own government, military, and citizens.

Despite their commitment to law, however, not all Israelis have respected the rule of law or the principles of democracy, as evidenced by the idol smashing of radical Zionists such as Rabbi Meir Kahane, who attended the same high school as I did and then became both a lawyer and a rabbi. In the late 1960s, he founded the Jewish Defense League (JDL), which espoused and practiced violence against enemies of the Jewish people, including the Soviet Union and anti-Israel Arabs.

Kahane believed that he was acting in the spirit of Abraham, the idol smasher, as well as other idol-smashing Jewish lawyers, such as Ze'ev Jabotinsky, Menachem Begin, and Yitzhak Shamir.

In the 1970s, several members of the JDL were placed on trial for the murder of a young Jewish woman who was accidentally killed when a smoke bomb was set off in the offices of Sol Hurok, a Jewish impresario who specialized in bringing Soviet entertainers to perform in the United States. The JDL disapproved of cultural exchanges with the Soviet Union, which was persecuting Jewish dissidents and refuseniks.

I successfully defended the JDL member who was accused of constructing the smoke bomb, and I became a hero of the JDL, despite my strong disapproval of its methods. I have written a detailed account of this case in *The Best Defense.*[11] Over the next several years, I debated Kahane on several occasions and represented him on free-speech matters.[12] The Supreme Court of Israel banned Kahane's party and sustained his expulsion from the Knesset on the ground that his racist views and advocacy of violence were inconsistent with the rule of law. He was assassinated by an Arab extremist in New York City in 1990.

It was my encounter with Meir Kahane and my fundamental disagreement with the unlawful and often violent means he employed to achieve just ends that contributed to my decision to become an advocate for Soviet Jewry and for the State of Israel and to try to follow more in the footsteps of the Abraham who argued on behalf of the sinners of Sodom than of the Abraham who shattered idols or the Abraham who was a fundamentalist.

## The Legal Advocate: Arguing with Authority

The legal advocate is different from the illegal idol shatterer. The advocate is committed to the rule of law. He or she would never knowingly violate the law or the Code of Professional Responsibility, though legal advocates might stretch the facts and the law in the interests of zealous advocacy and the rights of their clients, as Abraham did when he argued with God over the sinners of Sodom. But in doing so, the advocate remains respectful of the judge and the law, seeking to have the law applied in the interest of his client. The advocate has a stake in the law and is willing to preserve and improve it but not to denounce or destroy it. As Jesus put it, "Think not that I am come to destroy the law, or the prophets: I am not come to destroy, but to fulfil."[13] Among the greatest legal advocates in history have been many Jews; some—like Louis Brandeis—are well-known, others—like Max Hirschberg—less so.

## Louis Brandeis: The People's Lawyer

Louis Brandeis personified the Abrahamic lawyer who argued with God. He would deserve inclusion on any list of great Jewish lawyers—or of lawyers in general—even if he had never served with distinction as a justice on the U.S. Supreme Court. He was nominated to the high court because he was known as "the people's lawyer" who had devoted his distinguished career at the bar to protecting consumers, bank depositors, insurance holders, workers, and other ordinary citizens. His creation of the so-called Brandeis brief—which marshaled economic, sociological, and other empirical evidence in support of progressive legislation—revolutionized Supreme Court advocacy on behalf of the public interest. He, like Abraham, believed in arguing about numbers and in weighing costs and benefits. He also represented the rich and powerful, but generally in an effort to have them do the right thing. He called himself "counsel to the situation," and his goal was to solve problems in the public interest rather than to beat the other side.

Although his enemies regarded him as a radical, he was anything but an idol smasher. His temperament was judicial and nonconfrontational, and his style was gentle but firm. His counsel was sought by corporations, unions, banks, consumers, and politicians. He became an enormously successful and wealthy lawyer in a city in which anti-Semitism was rampant.

Brandeis's nomination to the Supreme Court by President Woodrow Wilson brought out the worst in America and in the elite bar. The legal establishment organized in opposition to his nomination, claiming its opposition was based on his radicalism rather than his Jewish heritage. The reality is that his perceived radicalism was based on anti-Semitic stereotyping. He was the first Jew appointed to the high court. (Judah Benjamin was twice offered a seat but declined.)

The leaders of the American Bar Association lined up solidly against the nomination. Six former association presidents, at the instigation of the incumbent president, Elihu Root, declared that Brandeis was "not a fit person" to sit on the Court.[14] The former president and future chief justice, William Howard Taft, dipped his "pen in vitriol [dispatching] letter after letter of calumny to friends and family, berating Brandeis for his ethics, politics, and religion."[15] Numerous local bar associations and individual elite lawyers alleged that Brandeis had a "defective standard of professional ethics."[16]

*The Wall Street Journal* declared, "In all the anti-corporation agitation of the past years one name stands out conspicuous above all others. Where others were radical he was rabid."[17] *The New York Times*, owned by a Jewish family, reported—without critique—on a petition to the Senate filed by the then president of Harvard, Lawrence Lowell,[18] and fifty-four others.[19] Beseeching the Senate not to confirm Brandeis's nomination, the signatories proclaimed, "We don't believe that Mr. Brandeis has the judicial temperament and capacity which should be required by a Judge of the Supreme Court."[20]

None of this was true of Brandeis the person. In fact, according to several lawyers who knew him, he had angered some clients by trying to be fair to both sides. But it reflected the stereotype of the Jewish idol-smashing lawyer, as idol smasher rather than dignified advocate.

George Wickersham, a former U.S. Attorney General and the president of the New York City Bar Association at the time, characterized Brandeis's supporters as "a bunch of Hebrew uplifters."[21] Taft complained that Brandeis was using his Judaism to curry political favor,[22] and Senator Henry Cabot Lodge opined that if Brandeis were not Jewish, "he would never have been appointed."[23] But Brandeis's support transcended religious and political grounds, especially among academics and practicing lawyers.

After a bruising confirmation battle, which included, for the first time, a public hearing by the Senate Judiciary Committee, Brandeis was confirmed by a vote of 47 to 27.[24] He went on to become one of the greatest Supreme Court justices in history, espousing a theory of cautious judicial restraint, especially when it came to striking down economic and social legislation, but being more activist in defense of free speech and due process. President Franklin Delano Roosevelt called him his "Isaiah" and frequently sought his judgment on important matters. He possessed an ideal judicial temperament.

Both before and after becoming a justice, Brandeis was an ardent Zionist leader who strongly advocated a homeland for the Jewish people. Working largely behind the scenes, and contributing considerable personal financial assistance, he made the case for American support of the Zionist project—a project that was not popular among the Reform German Jews of his social class. Toward the end of his life, he struggled mightily, if unsuccessfully, against the British decision to close Palestine to Jews seeking asylum from Nazism.

In his multidimensional career, he combined all the positive elements of the Abrahamic lawyer. He argued with authority, employing nuance on behalf of the people he tried to rescue, the persecuted of Europe; he was a commercial lawyer par excellence; and he shattered idols in his quest for a Jewish homeland. On balance, Brandeis certainly ranks as the greatest Jewish lawyer in American history. He should also be included on any short list of the greatest American lawyers, regardless of religious or ethnic background.

Brandeis's remarkable tenure as a justice established what came to be known as "the Jewish seat" on the Supreme Court. Following Brandeis came Benjamin Cardozo, Felix Frankfurter, Arthur Goldberg, Abe Fortas, Ruth Bader Ginsburg, Stephen Breyer, and Elena Kagan. At the time of this writing, the high court, which used to comprise white Protestant males, with an occasional Catholic, now has three Jewish and six Catholic justices, three of them women and one of them black. Almost no one today seems to care whether a justice or lawyer is Jewish. That was certainly not the case when Max Hirschberg practiced in Weimar Germany in the 1920s.


## Max Hirschberg: Truth to Power

A remarkable man who stood somewhere between Abraham the idol smasher and Abraham the defense attorney was the anti-Nazi lawyer Max Hirschberg.

Hirschberg was a liberal, secular Jewish lawyer in Weimar Germany who argued against the emergence of Nazism and then against the Nazi regime itself during Hitler's early period as chancellor of the Third Reich. His Jewish sensibilities, which came relatively late in life, were largely a reaction to the German anti-Semitism he experienced following World War I.

Even before the election of 1932, it was a daunting task to oppose Nazism, because the Weimar judiciary was extremely right-wing and many of the judges were openly sympathetic to Hitler and his party.[25] It was an even more daunting task to defend justice after the Nazis came to power, when the price of losing—or winning—was a one-way trip to Dachau.

Max Hirschberg was "the premier courtroom lawyer in Munich during the Weimar Republic," litigating the most important political cases during that period.[26] Weimar Germany boasted of its judiciary and of its commitment to the rule of law. Echoing Abraham's challenge to God— "Shall not the Judge of all the earth deal justly?"—Hirschberg repeatedly dared Bavarian judges to "uphold the rule of law," which they proclaimed loudly but applied rarely in political cases.[27]

Hirschberg's first major case involved a young Social Democrat named Felix Fechenbach, who had been accused of treason.[28] Characterized as "the German Dreyfus affair," it was the first of several treason prosecutions against critics of the quickly rising Nazi Party. The defendant was convicted, but his sentence was commuted, and he was released from prison on the same day that Hitler was freed—thus making the political nature of the case clear.

During the Weimar years, Hirschberg defended journalists, political activists, and ordinary defendants against what he believed were miscarriages of justice. He was also involved in a case against some of Hitler's thugs for starting street brawls. He was despised by Hitler and his followers not only because he was Jewish but also because he had confronted them in court and in the press.

When Hitler assumed power on January 30, 1933, everything changed. Hirschberg's name had long appeared on "right-wing murder lists,"[29] but now these lists were being used by the state to select its targets. Within weeks, Hitler suspended the constitution and declared an emergency, empowering the Gestapo to become police, judges, and executioners.

Among the first of many Jewish lawyers arrested under the new legal regime was Hirschberg, who was taken from his home at 4:30 in the morning and placed in "protective custody."[30] He was also subjected to disbarment proceedings. But like Abraham, who survived Nimrod's decree consigning him to the flames, Hirschberg miraculously survived the inferno of Nazism. He won his freedom and his ability to continue to practice law, albeit on a limited basis.

It soon became clear that neither he nor any other Jewish lawyer could help achieve justice in Nazi Germany, so again like Abraham he left the country of his birth and immigrated to a promised land, the United States (after a brief sojourn in Italy). He was too old to study for and seek admission to the bar in his new home, so he wrote about his experiences in Germany, especially about the mischarges of justice against which he had so bravely fought for so many years. He died in 1964 at the age of eighty, having argued against the most powerful and evil authority of his age. The wrongs that lawyers like Hirschberg fought against became the basis for new rights recognized following the Nazi era. The Jewish lawyer most responsible for developing these new rights is our next subject.

### René Cassin and the Invention of "Human Rights"

Most contemporary activists claim to support "human rights," but when one looks closely at what they are advocating, it often turns out to be "rights for me, but not for thee." Gay rights activists call their program the Human Rights Campaign, but that campaign is limited to the rights of homosexuals. Feminists likewise claim the mantle of human rights, but their emphasis is on one half of humanity. The Anti-Defamation League describes itself as a human rights organization, but its priority is the rights of Jews.[31] The same is true of "human rights" groups that care only about the Palestinians, the Kurds, the Tibetans, or the Tatars.

Abraham was the first human rights lawyer, arguing on behalf of justice for strangers—for thee, not for me. He knew that the family of his nephew Lot would be spared, but that was not enough. He wanted justice for all the people of Sodom. Indeed, several commentators have suggested that the reason he did not argue with God over the life of his own son is that he had too great a personal interest—and thus a bias—because of his love for Isaac.

To be an advocate of "human rights" requires going beyond one's particular group. A Jew who fights only against anti-Semitism is an advocate for *particular* rights, as is an African American who struggles only against racism, a woman who opposes only sexism, or a gay person who fights only homophobia. These are commendable activities, but they do not qualify as advocacy of *human* rights. Just as being a First Amendment advocate requires the active defense of expression one deplores, so too joining the "Human Rights Club" requires an active commitment to the universal rights of *all* people, even those one disagrees with or despises. The membership rolls of both "clubs" are, tragically, quite small under these criteria, though many claim their honorific mantles.

Being a member of the "Human Rights Club" does not require abstaining from advocacy for one's own group (however defined). It does not require sacrificing one's own child, as Abraham was willing to do. But it does require universal advocacy as well. The motto for the club might well be the famous dictum of the Jewish sage Hillel: "If I am not for myself, who will be for me? But if I am for myself alone, what am I? And if not now, when?"[32]

The lawyer who has most represented a commitment to universal human rights in modern times is René Cassin, who won the Nobel Peace Prize in 1968 for his work as the primary drafter of the Universal Declaration of Human Rights.[33] Born to a Jewish family in France, he remained an ardent Zionist throughout his life—a life committed to universal human rights. Many of his relatives were killed during the Holocaust, and he was a staunch opponent of anti-Semitism and other forms of racism and bigotry.

Cassin was a law professor and a government lawyer who achieved distinction in many areas of the law, but his greatest contribution was the promotion of human rights and the drafting of the Universal Declaration. Near the end of his life, he issued the following challenge: "Now that we possess an instrument capable of lifting or easing the burden of oppression and injustice in the world, we must learn to use it."[34]

Unfortunately, we have not. The Universal Declaration of Human Rights and the mechanisms created to implement it, especially at the United Nations, have been turned into instruments of oppression and injustice, especially against the State of Israel, which Cassin loved and admired.

The sad reality is that the inversion of the human rights agenda, especially at the UN, has needlessly cost many innocent lives. Since the time the world promised "never again" at the end of World War II and built a structure and jurisprudence designed to fulfill that important promise, another six million innocent victims of preventable genocides have been slaughtered while the world once again stood silent.

Cambodia, Rwanda, and Darfur are just the beginning of the story. The UN also has failed to help desperate civilians in Burundi, the former Yugoslavia, Syria, and other countries. While ignoring the gruesome killings by the member states in its midst, the United Nations has focused its time and attention on a single country—Israel. Its constituent bodies—especially the General Assembly and the Human Rights Council—have condemned Israel more frequently and more harshly than all the other nations of the world combined. This despite the documented fact that no nation facing comparable threats has ever killed *fewer* enemy civilians in its efforts to protect its own civilians.

The UN's obsession with Israel is not necessarily the only cause of its inaction on genocide, but it is certainly a contributing factor. Like all institutions, the United Nations has limited resources. When it dedicates so many of those resources to condemning and delegitimizing Israel, it decreases its ability to respond effectively to genocide. It is important to realize that the sheer amount of time the UN spends chastising Israel in one-sided and repetitive resolutions is also time *not* spent on preventing or at least condemning genocide.

What might have been if, *during* the Cambodian genocide, the General Assembly had passed a single resolution on Pol Pot's atrocities instead of wasting time debating whether Zionism was racism? How would the situation in Darfur have changed if, during its 2006–2007 sessions, the General Assembly had even once condemned the genocide in Sudan instead of passing nearly two dozen resolutions condemning Israel?

One might dismiss the UN's obsession with Israel if the body's failure to prevent suffering was not so serious. The UN could have intervened more quickly and vigorously and saved millions of lives during ongoing genocides. It is a broken institution. And until it ends its obsession with Israel, the UN cannot be fixed. Even some of its top officials recognize this reality, but their hands are tied, because anti-Israel (and anti-American) countries constitute a majority of the UN membership, thus giving anti-Israel resolutions an automatic majority.

The UN will remain a key facilitator—through its actions and inactions—of the tragic inversion of human rights that has characterized its work over the past forty years.

The real victims of this inversion have not been Israel or the other Western democracies that have been the focus of the UN condemnations. The real victims have been those willfully ignored by the UN, which has used its focus on Israel and other democracies as an excuse—a cover—for its malignant inaction against horrible human wrongs committed by the tyrannical regimes that control much of the UN agenda and give themselves exculpatory immunity from any UN condemnation or intervention. "Never again" has been turned into "again and again and again." The label of "human rights" has been used to promote human wrongs. The heroes of the human rights movement—René Cassin, Eleanor Roosevelt, Albert Schweitzer—should be turning over in their graves, as the shields they constructed to protect the helpless from oppression and genocide have been beaten into swords to be used to facilitate these human wrongs.[35]

One human wrong that has been redressed in recent years, though certainly not completely, is sexism. Among the Jewish lawyers who have promoted the legal aspects of feminism is Ruth Bader Ginsburg.

## Ruth Bader Ginsburg and the Development of Women's Rights

Following World War II, many Jewish lawyers became deeply involved in human rights, civil liberties, civil rights, and women's rights. Many of the leaders of these movements were Jewish lawyers, such as Jack Greenberg, who headed the NAACP Legal Defense Fund; Nadine Strossen, who was president of the American Civil Liberties Union; and Leonard Boudin, a founder of the National Emergency Civil Liberties Committee and the National Lawyers Guild.

Perhaps the most influential of these lawyers, who argued with the government in the spirit of Abraham's argument with God, was Ruth Bader Ginsburg.[36] She also followed in the footsteps of the biblical Deborah, the first Jewish woman to become a judge.[37]

Ginsburg was born in Brooklyn, where her family attended services at the East Midwood Jewish Center. She began her legal studies in 1956 at Harvard, where she was one of only nine women students in a class of more than five hundred men. When her husband secured employment in New York, she transferred to Columbia Law School and graduated at the top of her class. Despite her extraordinary record, she could not get a job in a major law firm.[38]

In 1963, Ginsburg became a law professor at Rutgers, where she edited the *Women's Rights Law Reporter*. She moved to Columbia Law School in 1972, where she edited a casebook on sex discrimination. She also helped to establish the Women's Rights Project and became general counsel of the ACLU.

In her position with the ACLU, Ginsburg litigated some of the most important women's rights cases in the Supreme Court. She developed and employed a somewhat controversial tactic in her effort to expand the rights of women: she often used cases involving the rights of *men* to establish *principles* that would be equally applicable to *women*.

In 1980, President Jimmy Carter appointed Ginsburg to the U.S. Court of Appeals for the District of Columbia, on which she served until President Bill Clinton nominated her to the Supreme Court in 1993. In announcing her nomination, this is what he said:

As I told Judge Ginsburg last night when I called to ask her to accept the nomination, I decided on her for three reasons. First, in her years on the bench she has genuinely distinguished herself as one of our Nation's best judges, progressive in outlook, wise in judgment, balanced and fair in her opinions. Second, over the course of a lifetime, in her pioneering work in behalf of the women of this country, she has compiled a truly historic record of achievement in the finest traditions of American law and citizenship. And finally, I believe that in the years ahead she will be able to be a force for consensus-building on the Supreme Court, just as she has been on the Court of Appeals, so that our judges can become an instrument of our common unity in the expression of their fidelity to the Constitution. . . .

It is important to me that Judge Ginsburg came to her views and attitudes by doing, not merely by reading and studying. Despite her enormous ability and academic achievements, she could not get a job with a law firm in the early 1960s because she was a woman and the mother of a small child. Having experienced discrimination, she devoted the next twenty years of her career to fighting it and making this country a better place for our wives, our mothers, our sisters, and our daughters. She herself argued and won many of the women's rights cases before the Supreme Court in the 1970s. Many admirers of her work say that she is to the women's movement what former Supreme Court Justice Thurgood Marshall was to the movement for the rights of African Americans. I can think of no greater compliment to bestow on an American lawyer.[39]

The comparison was not entirely apt, because Marshall had to endure threats on his life as he litigated an unpopular cause in hostile parts of our nation, whereas Ginsburg was litigating an increasingly popular cause in a far less hostile environment; but she was a pioneer and helped advance the role of women through her skills as a litigator.

Justice Ginsburg has served on the high court for more than twenty-one years, generally aligning herself with the moderate-liberal wing on most issues. Her closest friend has been Antonin Scalia, a fellow New York and opera lover who has been the leader of the conservative wing. Justice Ginsburg has been honored by several Jewish organizations and has remained committed to both her Jewish and her feminist values. But above all she has been a lawyer and a judge who has followed the biblical command to pursue justice.

Another lawyer who followed this command at the risk of his own life was a committed Catholic who belongs on any list of righteous lawyers.

## Jan Karski

This book is about Jewish lawyers. But I must include one non-Jewish lawyer because, though a Catholic, he was more "Jewish" than almost any lawyer of his day. I include him also to contrast him with a certain Jewish lawyer who will always be remembered for what he failed to do. The name of the non-Jew was Jan Karski,[40] and he shattered idols and argued with authority in the highest tradition of Abraham. This is Karski's remarkable, tragic, and uplifting story.[41]

In the early 1940s, Karski, a Polish Catholic who had recently graduated from the Lvov law school, was a member of the Polish underground. He repeatedly risked his life to tell the world of the Nazi horrors being inflicted on Polish Jewry. Karski volunteered twice to enter the Warsaw Ghetto disguised as a Jew so that he could recount his eyewitness observations to a skeptical world.[42] He also agreed to be smuggled into the Jewish death camp at Belzec, dressed in an Estonian guard uniform. What he saw, heard, and smelled was beyond imagining. He recorded every detail in his lawyer's memory: numbers, locations, methods. This is some of what he recorded at Belzec:

> Alternately swinging and firing with their rifles, the policemen were forcing still more people into the two cars which were already overfull. The shots continued to ring out in the rear and the driven mob surged forward, exerting an irresistible pressure against those nearest the train. . . .

These were helpless since they had the weight of the entire advancing throng against them and responded only with howls of anguish to those who, clutching at their hair and clothes for support, trampling on necks, faces and shoulders, breaking bones and shouting with insensate fury, attempted to clamber over them. After the cars had already been filled beyond normal capacity, more than another score of human beings, men, women and children gained admittance in this fashion. Then the policemen slammed the doors across the hastily withdrawn limbs that still protruded and pushed the iron bars in place. . . .

All this while the entire camp had reverberated with a tremendous volume of sound in which the hideous groans and screams mingled weirdly with shots, curses, and bellowed commands. . . .

The floors of the car had been covered with a thick, white powder. It was quicklime. . . . The moist flesh coming in contact with the lime is rapidly dehydrated and burned. The occupants of the cars would be literally burned to death before long, the flesh eaten from their bones. . . . Secondly, the lime would prevent decomposing bodies from spreading disease. . . .

It was twilight when the forty-six (I counted them) cars were packed. . . . From one end to the other, the train, with its quivering cargo of flesh, seemed to throb, vibrate, rock, and jump as if bewitched. . . . Inside the camp a few score dead bodies remained and a few in the final throes of death. German policemen walked around at leisure with smoking guns, pumping bullets into anything that, by a moan or motion, betrayed an excess of vitality. Soon, not a single one was left alive.[43]

After Karski completed his extraordinarily risky visits to the Jewish ghetto and death camp, he was captured by the Gestapo and tortured. He escaped, changed his appearance to avoid recapture, and again risked his life traveling secretly through occupied Europe to America to try to persuade our government to rescue Jews from the emerging Holocaust. The ambassador of the Polish government in exile arranged a meeting between Karski and Justice Felix Frankfurter, who was one of President Roosevelt's most trusted intimates. The purpose of the meeting was to convince Frankfurter that the reports of genocide, which were filtering out of occupied Eastern Europe, were true and that he should communicate that truth to the president.

In the 1980s, I met with Karski, who was then teaching at Georgetown University, and he recalled his meeting with Frankfurter: "One does not forget such an encounter. Every word is emblazoned in my memory." Karski told Frankfurter precisely what he had seen with his own eyes. After Karski spoke uninterrupted for forty-five minutes, providing a detailed first-person account of the Warsaw Ghetto and the extermination camp at Belzec, Frankfurter stood up and began to pace back and forth. Karski recalled, "He seemed to be passing judgment on whether I was telling the truth." He had been warned that Frankfurter was "an extremely pompous man who demands respect, if not subservience." Karski waited as the justice paced. Then Frankfurter stopped and looked Karski straight in the eye and said, "A man like me talking to a man like you must be totally honest. So I am. So I say, I cannot believe you."

The Polish ambassador who had accompanied me was flabbergasted: "Felix, how can you say such a thing? You know he is saying the truth. He was checked and rechecked in London and here. Felix, what are you saying?"

Frankfurter responded, "I did not say that he was lying. I said that I cannot believe him. There is a difference. My mind, my heart, they are made in such a way that I cannot conceive it."

Karski told me that to that day—nearly fifty years later—he did not understand Frankfurter's purported distinction. He suspected that deep down Frankfurter probably knew that he was hearing a truthful account of the horrors confronting Polish Jewry. Why, Karski asked rhetorically, would a Polish Catholic exaggerate what was happening to the Jews?

But Karski thought that Frankfurter was afraid to acknowledge what he believed, because that would require him to convince others of the truth of Karski's unfathomable image of hell on earth. The justice and presidential adviser was concerned that others, especially Roosevelt, would not believe what he believed, thereby damaging his credibility on other issues and in other areas.

Frankfurter did not want to be regarded as one of those softhearted Jews who put Jewish lives before the American war effort. He did not want to endanger his valuable credibility with the president over an issue of Jewish sentimentality. And so he said nothing and did nothing as millions of his brothers and sisters—and their children—were slaughtered.[44]

David S. Wyman, in his monumental work *The Abandonment of the Jews*, put it this way:

> Supreme Court Justice Felix Frankfurter had regular access to Roosevelt during the war, and he exercised a quiet but powerful influence in many sectors of the administration. Although he used his contacts to press numerous policies and plans, rescue [of the Jews] was not among them.[45]

The historian Jerold S. Auerbach is no kinder to Frankfurter:

> He concerned himself with affairs in India, Australia, and Vichy, France. Yet Frankfurter would not utilize his position and contacts, or his irrepressible energy, in the service of Jewish needs during the most desperate years of Jewish history. Among the varied causes that engaged his extrajudicial efforts, the rescue of Jews from the Holocaust was not among them. . . . [N]othing was more characteristic of American Jews [like Frankfurter and others near the center of power] than their acquiescence in Roosevelt's "abandonment of the Jews" of Europe. Proximity to power . . . all but silenced them to Jewish tragedy.[46]

The same can be said—to a greater or lesser extent—of most other Jewish political leaders and presidential intimates of that era, such as Herbert Lehman, Samuel Rosenman, David Niles, Bernard Baruch, and Rabbi Stephen Wise. Only Henry Morgenthau can be counted as a highly placed friend of President Roosevelt who was prepared to risk his credibility over a Jewish issue. This is a shameful record of inaction that must never be repeated.

No American Jew today wants his or her epitaph to read—as Felix Frankfurter's must always read in Jewish history—"He could have helped, but didn't. He could have believed, but wouldn't. He placed his own interests before those of his fellow Jews." I was the Felix Frankfurter Professor of Law at Harvard for more than two decades. I would often tell my students, over lunch or dinner, the Karski-Frankfurter story as an object lesson in how not to live one's life. My generation of Jewish Americans lives with the dread that we may be the next generation's Felix Frankfurters—that we may be denying the reality of emerging threats to the security, and indeed survival, of large segments of Jewry in Israel and other parts of the world. It is the tragic memory of these and many similar stories of the failure of Jewish lawyers and leaders during our darkest period that has inspired future generations to be aggressive on behalf of Soviet, Ethiopian, Syrian, and other endangered Jews. Perhaps that is why we are so unified in our support of Israeli security while differing on other aspects of Middle Eastern policy. We would rather err on the side of incautious action than cautious inaction. Felix Frankfurter preserved his reputation as a cautious Jewish leader who never cried wolf—even when the wolf was slaughtering his brothers and sisters. While my generation does not want to dilute the credibility of our cries for help, we sound the alarm when we see, or smell, the first evidence of smoke. We are prepared to shout "Fire!" in a crowded theater if we believe there is a substantial possibility that the theater is, in fact, beginning to burn. We recognize the risks of being too thin-skinned, but we know the dangers of being too lethargic. As a people who came close to having no future, we guard our future as if it were the present.

That is why it is proper to include Jan Karski as an honorary Jewish lawyer who was prepared to risk his life to protect the Jews of Poland. In doing so, he followed in the footsteps of the Abraham who broke idols and argued with God about his injustice. Frankfurter too followed in the footsteps of Abraham—the Abraham who refused to question God's immoral command to sacrifice his son Isaac.[47] It is to those Jewish lawyers who failed to stand up to immorality that we now turn.

## Collaborators, Facilitators, and Court Jews:
## Abrahamic Lawyers Who Accept Immoral Commands
## from Authority Figures

The Abraham who arose early to obey God's immoral command to sacrifice his son also has a long—if not always distinguished—list of followers. In addition to Justice Felix Frankfurter and his ilk—prominent Jews with access to power who refused to risk their access by arguing on behalf of Jews in trouble with the powerful—there have always been official "court Jews."

These Jews—lawyers, rabbis, lay leaders, and ordinary people—have decided that the best way to get along was to go along. Some blindly accepted the commands of kings, dictators, and other rulers. Others blindly followed their rabbis or community leaders. Yes, we have often been a stiff-necked people, but too often we have also been a weak-kneed people, unwilling to challenge authority or to refuse immoral commands. Of course there are classic Jewish jokes about this phenomenon, including the one about the two Jews about to be executed by a czarist firing squad. The Jews are offered the traditional blindfolds, which the first one bravely rejects. The second warns him, "Don't make trouble."

Some of these "Don't make trouble" Jews became collaborators in all sorts of evils, from the Inquisition, to Nazism, to Stalinism, to anti-Zionism, to McCarthyism. I will never forget a conversation I had with the late Roy Cohn, the Jewish lawyer who became one of Senator Joseph McCarthy's henchmen and one of the persecutors of American Communists and fellow travelers, many of whom were Jewish. Toward the end of his life, Cohn worked with me on the Claus von Bülow case; he represented Claus's daughter, who had been cut off from inheriting part of her mother's fortune because she sided with Claus against her half siblings.

I didn't raise the issue of his sordid role in the McCarthyism witch hunts, but Cohn apparently felt the need to justify what he had done. He explained that it was important to him, as an anti-Communist Jew, to play a highly visible role in the campaign against American Communists, precisely because so many Jews had become Communists during the 1930s, when Communism was seen by many as the best weapon against Nazism. "I didn't want American Christians to believe that Communism was a Jewish thing," he told me. "I wanted them to see that a Jew named Cohn was on their side, fighting against the evils of Communism."

Whether this was an after-the-fact rationalization for his own careerist and/or opportunistic motivations, I'm sure he came to believe it, as did other Jews who collaborated with Nazism by becoming heads of the *Judenräte* or who collaborated with Stalinism by becoming the purveyors of Soviet anti-Semitism. After the fall of the Soviet Union, I met with a Moscow Jewish lawyer who had been at the forefront of defending the Kremlin against charges of anti-Semitism. He acknowledged to me that he had lied about the situation of Soviet Jews but argued vociferously that he did it to help his Jewish brothers and sisters. "I had access to the Kremlin," he assured me. "And I used my access to help many individual Jews in small ways." He too believed that his collaboration with immorality had served the interests of his fellow Jews more than the strident demonstrations that dissident Jews and refuseniks had conducted, which served only—in his view—"to antagonize the party leaders."

Although it is difficult to judge these and other collaborators without having stood in their shoes, history has not been kind to most of them. The problems they faced were often complex, and it is hard for later generations to understand their situations fully.

Perhaps the best example of the difficulty of judging leaders retrospectively is the situation faced by Jewish leaders during the 1930s and 1940s both in the United States and in Europe. American Jews, for the most part, loved President Roosevelt and repeatedly voted for him. In my home, a picture of "President Rosenfelt," as my grandmother pronounced it, hung on the wall, as it did on the walls of many Jewish homes. Roosevelt cultivated Jewish advisers, many of whom were lawyers who formed part of the "brain trust" that helped him implement the New Deal. Felix Frankfurter, Samuel Rosenman, Benjamin Cohen, James Warburg, and Henry Morgenthau were close to Roosevelt during the critical period when much more could have been done to rescue the Jews of Europe. Among the group of Roosevelt intimates, only Secretary of the Treasury Henry Morgenthau, the sole nonlawyer among them, was willing to risk his access to the president by challenging his inaction.

Frankfurter's unwillingness to introduce Jan Karski to Roosevelt was only one of many failures on the part of American Jewish leaders—especially lawyers and rabbis—to smash idols or even to argue forcefully with authority in the tradition of the early Abraham. Instead, they appeared willing to sacrifice their European brothers and sisters in order to show their faith in the Roosevelt strategy of keeping our gates closed to refugees so as not to alienate his anti-Semitic supporters in Congress, in the State Department, and among the general public.

Only Morgenthau, among the Jewish government officials, complained loudly and frequently, eventually persuading Roosevelt to create the U.S. War Refugee Board, which saved many Jewish lives toward the end of the war.

It may be difficult for contemporary Americans to put themselves in the position of Jewish leaders during the 1930s and 1940s. The Jewish community was relatively powerless and vulnerable. Anti-Semitism was not only pervasive but politically and socially acceptable. President Roosevelt's cousin Laura Delano Houghteling—who happened to be the wife of the U.S. immigration commissioner—opposed allowing Jewish children into America during the Holocaust, reportedly warning that "20,000 charming children would all too soon grow into 20,000 ugly adults."[48] Elected officials felt comfortable referring to Jews as "kikes" and making other openly anti-Semitic remarks on the floor of Congress.[49] A religious leader such as Father Charles Coughlin railed against "the Jews" during his popular weekly radio broadcasts.[50] America's most influential industrialist, Henry Ford, wrote articles and books blaming our problems on "the international Jew."[51] Charles Lindbergh, America's most beloved hero, had positive things to say about Hitler and negative things to say about Jews.[52]

Jews had little influence on politics, the economy, and public opinion. Even in aspects of American life in which individual Jews were dominant—the newly emerging motion picture business, radio, and some newspapers—they were reluctant to appear to be serving the interests of their co-religionists. The few motion pictures that dealt openly with Jewish issues—such as *Gentleman's Agreement*[53]—were produced largely by non-Jews. *The New York Times*, which was owned by the Sulzberger family, buried stories of Nazi atrocities toward the Jews. And most of the Jewish financiers, who made money for themselves, seemed to care little about the Jews of Europe.[54]

During the run-up to World War II, some of those most strongly opposed to America's entry into another "European conflict" blamed the Jews for "pushing" Roosevelt into helping England. Jewish leaders believed they had to act discreetly and cautiously, *following* rather than trying to *lead* the way. They condemned those, like Peter Bergson, who led demonstrations and public opposition to Roosevelt's policies.

In retrospect, this may look like cowardice or craven efforts at currying favor with a popular leader, but at the time it appeared to many leaders to be prudent. Perhaps history will judge it to be a little of both.

If the situation of American Jews, who lived far away from the death camps of Europe, is difficult to judge in retrospect, how much more difficult is it to sit in judgment over those Jews—some of whom were lawyers—who were placed in positions of responsibility by the Nazis? The various *Judenälteste* (elders of the Jews) who were put in charge of the *Ältestenräte* (counsels of elders) or the *Judenräte* had to balance the prospect of saving some Jews against the demand by the Nazis for Jewish victims. Looked at in retrospect, such collaboration with evil is difficult to comprehend, because in the end so few lives were saved. But viewed from the perspective of the times, the motives of such collaborators become possible to understand, if not to justify.

Everything changed after the war, when Jews became more assertive, first during the civil rights movement, then in support of Israel and Soviet Jewry. But my generation, which is credited with being more proactive, had it much easier than our parents' generation. We were financially more secure, politically more influential, and socially more accepted. We had learned from their experience that prudence needed to be backed with power, discretion needed to be supported by determination, and quiet diplomacy needed to carry the threat of noisy demonstrations and economic reprisals.

For our parents' generation, the model was the compliant Abraham who was prepared to sacrifice his child to demonstrate his faith in a powerful God. Some in that generation stood silently by the blood of their co-religionists for prudential reasons, others because they believed it was God's will, and still others because they were frightened. For our generation, the model was the contentious Abraham who argued with God on behalf of justice for people in distant places and the Abraham who rescued his nephew Lot. For some, like Meir Kahane, it was the Abraham who shattered his father's idols.

In the early days of American history, the great moral issue did not directly involve Jews—though Jews played roles on both sides of the conflict. That issue, of course, was slavery. Judah Benjamin, the greatest Jewish lawyer of his day, not only collaborated with this evil by owning slaves but became one of the most forceful defenders of the Confederacy.

## Judah Benjamin:
### From Confederate Leader to Commercial Lawyer

Judah Benjamin was truly a lawyer for many seasons.[55] He was born in the West Indies to British Jewish parents—Sephardic Jews whose families came from Spain. As an infant, he was brought to the United States, where his family settled in my wife's hometown of Charleston, South Carolina. His father was a founder of the first and oldest reform synagogue in the United States, where my wife was confirmed.

After leaving (or being expelled from)[56] Yale College before completing a degree, he "read for the law"—as was the traditional way of becoming a lawyer in those days—and moved to New Orleans, where he married a Creole woman, bought a sugar plantation, and owned slaves. His law practice thrived, as did his political career.

A decade before the Civil War, he sold his plantation and his 150 slaves and turned to politics full-time. He was selected by the state legislature to serve in the U.S. Senate—the second Jew to achieve that status, the first having been his cousin David Levy Yulee of Florida.[57] Shortly thereafter, he was offered a seat on the U.S. Supreme Court by President Millard Fillmore, which he declined. A few years later, President Franklin Pierce proposed his nomination to the high court. Again he declined, preferring to advocate in the Senate for his beloved South in the run-up to what would soon become the War Between the States. Because of his strong support for slavery, Senator Benjamin Wade of Ohio labeled him a "Hebrew with Egyptian principles,"[58] an apt characterization.

When the South seceded from the Union, Jefferson Davis appointed Judah Benjamin to be first the attorney general and later secretary of war and secretary of state. He was called the "brains of the Confederacy" and one of its most articulate oratorical defenders. He advocated the freeing of any slave who agreed to fight for the Confederacy.

After Lee's surrender at Appomattox, Benjamin—fearing a treason charge—escaped to England, where he established himself as one of the leading commercial lawyers of his day. Following in the footsteps of Abraham, he first specialized in real estate transactions and wrote the leading treatise on the law of sales—a book that is still regarded as a bible of sales law.[59] He earned a fortune as a British commercial lawyer and used some of it to help support his Confederate friends, including Jefferson Davis.

It is difficult to categorize Judah Benjamin. He surely was a Jewish lawyer, though his association with his heritage diminished following his marriage to a Catholic woman.[60] His Jewish background did not seem to hold him back in the South, though his enemies in the North made much of it. He collaborated with evil, as did many southerners—including Thomas Jefferson, long before the Civil War—though they probably believed they were on the right side of history. Abraham too owned slaves. Indeed, southern religious leaders, in their effort to justify slavery from a theological perspective, often pointed to "the Abrahamic family," which included slaves, and to those parts of the Bible that set out the rules for dealing with slaves in a "just" manner.[61] In a pamphlet titled

*A Defence of Southern Slavery Against the Attacks of Henry Clay and Alexander Campbell*, by a "Southern Clergyman," the following "argument" was offered:

> Did not God intend the Jewish nation as his favorite and peculiar people, to exist in a well organized state of society? . . . We next ask him, if God did not incorporate with the Jewish polity, slavery, consisting in perpetual bondage? What is remarkable too [is that] it was negro slavery, or the bondage of the Canaanitish descendants of Ham, whom God authorized to be held in hereditary bondage under the laws of the Jewish polity. Leviticus xxv. 45. Again we ask Mr. Clay . . . whether God, in his infinite goodness, did not see that slavery would be a blessing both to the master and servant as the ground of his appointment of the institution amongst his chosen people? And if he had seen slavery to be a social and moral evil, would he not have inflicted a curse, and not a blessing upon the nation whom it was his intention to bless? We ask, further, whether, if the omniscient God did not know that the institution of slavery would, in its character and influence, tend to the preservation of true liberty, civil and religious, among the Jews, would he have incorporated it into their government?[62]

The clergyman specifically cited the case of Lot's "recapture" from the four kings by Abraham's 318 "slaves" as evidence that slavery could help in "the preservation of liberty."[63] I don't know if Judah Benjamin agreed with this biblical justification for slavery, but it is clear that history has correctly rejected these absurd biblical defenses of a deeply immoral institution.

Judah Benjamin must be judged as an accomplished lawyer by the standards of his day. He was brilliant, energetic, and devoted to his clients and causes, but he was on the wrong side of history, and history is, and should be, unforgiving when it comes to a moral issue as critical as slavery. Like Abraham, Benjamin listened to the wrong voice when it came to the most important moral issue of his time.

## Bruno Kreisky: The Jewish Lawyer Who Admired Nazis and Palestinian Terrorists

Another Jewish lawyer who failed the test of morality was the Austrian chancellor Bruno Kreisky. Although he would have disclaimed the noble title of Jewish lawyer, he warrants inclusion because he used his Jewish heritage as both a sword and a shield in the interest of ignoble causes.

As a young socialist politician, Kreisky was forced by the Gestapo to leave Austria during the Nazi period. Although he never formally renounced his Jewish heritage, he did everything in his power to distance himself from Jewish values and Jewish issues. He described Judaism as the "fossilized ghetto offshoot of a disbursed ethno-religious group lack[ing] any national characteristics." He was a virulent anti-Zionist who became the first European leader to support Yasser Arafat, even when Arafat was actively promoting terrorism against Jewish civilians in Europe and around the world. He was also a strong supporter of Muammar Gaddafi, calling him and Arafat "freedom fighters" while characterizing the Israeli prime minister Menachem Begin as a "terrorist."

Kreisky denied the right of the Jewish people to nationhood, and he equated Zionism with the racial ideology of Nazism. But he tried to maintain cordial relations with Israeli socialists.

In order to achieve high office in Austria, Kreisky had to become an apologist for former (and some not so former) Nazis. He occasionally used anti-Semitic code words in his efforts to curry favor with Austria's far-right nationalists and neo-Nazis such as Norbert Burger, who said he had no objection to Kreisky despite his Jewishness. Kreisky appointed several former Nazis to his cabinet.

Kreisky condemned the World Jewish Congress for raising the issue of Kurt Waldheim's hidden Nazi past. He also condemned the Nazi hunter Simon Wiesenthal, calling him a "Jewish fascist" and observing that "one finds reactionaries also among Jews, as well as thieves, murderers and prostitutes." Wiesenthal brought criminal charges against Kreisky for "malicious slander." Kreisky was convicted and received a three-year suspended sentence and a large fine—an example of yet another Jew on trial, but this time for his anti-Jewish statements.

Kreisky used his Jewishness as a tactic to legitimate his role as defender of Austria's Nazi past (as well as present). Many Austrians approved of the Jew who helped expiate and whitewash their notorious past. He is widely blamed for the fact that Austria, unlike Germany, never seriously confronted its Nazi legacy. It didn't have to. Instead, it elected a Jew—a Jew-hating, anti-Zionist Jew, to be sure, but a Jew by Hitler's definition—to its highest office.

Kreisky did not even have the excuse of the Jewish *Kapos* and Nazi collaborators during the Holocaust. He lived in Sweden during the Nazi period. He freely chose his role as facilitator of terrorism, apologist for Nazism, and hater of all things Jewish simply to earn the support of voters in the most anti-Semitic country of Europe.[64]

At the end of his life, he made some feeble efforts at *teshuva*—redemption. He tried to offer some help to Soviet Jews; he belatedly criticized Arafat and Waldheim; he referred to the numerous relatives he lost in the Holocaust. But history will remember him as a Jewish lawyer turned politician who exploited his Jewish heritage to lend credibility to his anti-Jewish actions. It will also remember him as a man who got along better with Nazis than with Zionists and who originated many of the worst libels against the nation-state of the Jewish people—including analogizing Israel to apartheid South Africa, Nazi Germany, and other fascist "police states."

The left-wing writer Peter Michael Lingens summarized Kreisky's lifetime ambition as "to be accepted by former Nazis."[65] He exceeded that ambition. He was accepted by *current* Nazis as well, as their "Golden Goy."[66]

## Rescuing Prisoners and Hostages

One of the most important mitzvoth (good deeds) of Judaism is *pidyon shvuim*, the rescue of hostages. Among the blessings Jews bestow on God is *matir assurim*, the redeemer of the imprisoned. When I helped Anatoly Sharansky achieve his freedom from the Soviet Gulag in 1986, the first words he whispered in my ear were "baruch matir assurim"—blessed are those who redeem the imprisoned. It was the best "legal fee" I ever received.[67]

Blessings don't arise in a vacuum but instead grow out of a historical context. Throughout history, Jews have been captured, taken as hostages, and falsely imprisoned. The first recorded instance of a Jewish rescuer of hostages is Abraham, who organized the military rescue of his nephew Lot. From that time, Jews have tried—not always with Abraham's success—to follow in the footsteps of the patriarch.

Among the Jews of the Chabad movement, one of the holiest days of the year is the nineteenth day of the Hebrew month of Kislev, on which Rabbi Shneur Zalman, the founder of the Lubavitcher movement, was released from his imprisonment by the czar on a trumped-up charge of treason.[68]

In my own family, we celebrate my paternal grandfather who rescued nearly thirty distant cousins who were trapped in Czechoslovakia on the eve of the Holocaust. Grandpa Louie secured false affidavits from friends and neighbors in Brooklyn, attesting to their need for rabbis, cantors, and other religious functionaries for the "synagogues" in their basements. The noble end of rescuing relatives—even distant ones—from evil justified the legally questionable means needed to achieve this mitzvah. Perhaps that is why I am so sympathetic to the so-called illegal immigrants who so desperately seek citizenship in our great country.

As a community, American Jews largely failed in our efforts to rescue European Jews from the horrors of Nazism, but we succeeded beyond all expectations in rescuing Soviet Jews from the oppression, discrimination, and de-Judaization that characterized life behind the Iron Curtain.

Among the "Abrahams" who rescued their "Lots" was my friend and colleague Professor Irwin Cotler, a Canadian Jew who, in the spirit of René Cassin, has devoted his life to rescuing Jews, and others, in captivity. We worked together in an effort to release Anatoly Sharansky and Nelson Mandela, with Cotler taking the laboring oar. He also took the lead in helping Jewish and other dissidents in far-flung parts of the world ranging from Argentina to Peru, Syria, China, Iran, Egypt, Indonesia, and South Africa.

During one of his trips to Moscow in 2006, Cotler was poisoned—by government officials, he believes—and became deathly ill. His symptoms were the same as those suffered by Alexander Litvinenko, who was almost certainly poisoned by the KGB. In March 2014, Cotler was included on a blacklist of thirteen prominent Canadians who were being denied entry to Russia. His response was, "I wear my exclusion from Russia as a badge of honour and am proud to be in such distinguished company. . . . I have no desire to visit Moscow and be poisoned as happened on my last trip."[69]

In the United States, he has been among the leaders in the effort to have the outrageously long sentence of Jonathan Pollard, who pleaded guilty to spying for Israel, commuted.

In my letter of nomination for the Nobel Peace Prize for Cotler, I argued that he has been a true human rights hero, in a "rights for thee, and not just for me" sense:

> More than any other lawyer in the world, Irwin Cotler has represented an apolitical, neutral approach to human rights. In an age when most alleged advocates for human rights are really advocates for a particular political or ideological agenda, Professor Cotler has rigorously defended the rights of individuals across the political, ideological, religious, racial, and ethnic spectrum. He has represented Arabs and Jews; Communists and anti-Communists; Westerners and Easterners and everyone in between. His advocacy sends a powerful and needed message that the human rights agenda must remain pure and should not be allowed to be hijacked in the interests of any particular group.

I have known Prof. Cotler for more than forty years and have been repeatedly amazed at the purity and consistency of his advocacy. He has devoted his life to those most in need of human rights advocacy, and he has done it without remuneration and without seeking personal recognition.

The concept of human rights is in great danger today of being trivialized and diluted. Every group claims to be defending human rights, even when they limit their advocacy to their own particular group, as most do. Claiming to be a human rights group gives false credibility to the particularistic claims of most groups. There is nothing wrong with being an advocate for women's rights, or an advocate for Black rights, or an advocate for Jewish rights, or an advocate for Palestinians' rights, or an advocate for Gay rights, or an advocate for Christian rights. But to be an advocate for human rights requires complete neutrality as to the substantive issues and the particular group that benefits or loses from a vindication of human rights.

Amnesty International could, at an early stage in its advocacy, claim to be a human rights organization. So could Human Rights Watch. So could others. Each of these organizations—yes, every one of them—has lost its credibility as a human rights organization, because it has taken sides politically, because it favors the rights of some groups over others, because its priorities reflect a strong bias, because its allocation of resources speaks more loudly than its claim to neutrality. Only Irwin Cotler stands above this partisan fray and defends the human rights of all, with no agenda other than the broadest possible and most neutral protections of all human rights.

For this, Prof. Cotler deserves the Nobel Peace Prize. Recognizing his unique role will send a powerful message that the human rights agenda should not be hijacked, diluted, or politicized by the hidden agendas of those who claim to be advocates for neutral human rights.[70]

Irwin Cotler displayed courage in traveling to dangerous parts of the world in his efforts to help the imprisoned, but he went with the protections afforded lawyers, diplomats, and public officials. Others, like Abraham and Jan Karski, undertook even greater risks, as did the young Jewish woman who went into the belly of the beast to try to rescue Hungarian Jews from the Nazis. Her name was Hannah Senesh.[71] She was part of a group of thirty-seven Jews who parachuted into Yugoslavia as part of an effort to cross the border into Hungary. She was not a lawyer—she was an accomplished poet—though some of her fellow rescuers had been law students before the war. She was caught and tortured for refusing to provide her captors with any information that might have led to the capture of her compatriots. She was then placed "on trial" and convicted of treason. She was executed by a firing squad shortly before the liberation of Hungary. She is now a national hero of the Jewish nation and the Jewish people.

Another Jew who died in the effort—this time successful—to rescue other Jews and non-Jews was Jonathan Netanyahu, who led the commando raid on Entebbe that freed more than a hundred hostages who had been hijacked by terrorists from the Popular Front for the Liberation of Palestine and the German Revolutionary Cells. Even before he was killed at Entebbe, Netanyahu had participated in several military operations that rescued hostages and military prisoners. Although neither Senesh nor Netanyahu was a lawyer, they deserve a place of honor on any list of heroes who followed in the tradition of the Abraham who risked his life to rescue his captured nephew.

When a group of Jewish Mossad agents were captured and imprisoned in Cyprus on charges of spying for Turkey—in fact, they were spying on Palestinian terrorists who were planning an attack against Israeli civilians—the head of the Mossad sought my assistance. After I helped to secure their release, he sent me the following letter:

I remember the energy you showed when we came to you seeking both advice and action. You threw yourself into the fray and showed every possible willingness to give us both your time and renowned counsel.

As you know, there is no greater "Mitzva" in Judaism than "Pidyon Shevuyim"—prisoner release. And nevertheless, not every person would be prepared to be associated with "one of us." So be it. You, for your part, acted in the best and noblest of our traditions.

We wish you well; we thank you for what you did and what you were willing to do. May we all live to see the day when a profession such as mine gives way to more pleasant occupations. There is still some way to go before this comes about.

Unfortunately, the need to secure Jews persists. Today, Jews are trapped in Iran, in Ethiopia, and in other parts of the world. Many Jews have recently fled from Venezuela, Ukraine, South Africa, and France. The ancient need for redeemers and sanctuaries is not only history. It is current events. That is why Israel's controversial law of return—a law that is inspired by Abraham's rescue and return of Lot—must continue to keep the doors open to Jews in need.

## In the Footsteps of Abraham the Deal Maker

Abraham's last legal action was to negotiate and buy the Cave of Machpelah and the surrounding fields as a final resting place for his late wife, Sarah. He insisted on paying a fair price—perhaps even over-paying a bit—so that the local residents would recognize his ownership in perpetuity.

Abraham the deal-making lawyer also lives in perpetuity through the thousands of Jewish commercial lawyers who have dominated the legal profession in so many cities around the world for so many years. The dominant role of the Jewish commercial lawyer is all the more remarkable in light of the discrimination Jewish lawyers have encountered over the years.

Here is an apt description of the situation in New York City in the 1940s and 1950s:

The old-line law firms of New York operated like a private club. They were all headquartered in downtown Manhattan, in and around Wall Street, in somber, granite-faced buildings. The partners at the top firms graduated from the same Ivy League schools, attended the same churches, and summered in the same oceanside towns on Long Island. They wore conservative gray suits. Their partnerships were known as "white-shoe" firms—in apparent reference to the white bucks favored at the country club or a cocktail party, and they were very particular in whom they hired. As Erwin Smigel wrote in *The Wall Street Lawyer*, his study of the New York legal establishment of that era, they were looking for

> lawyers who are Nordic, have pleasing personalities and "clean-cut" appearances, are graduates of the "right schools," have the "right" social background and experience in the affairs of the world, and are endowed with tremendous stamina. A former law school dean, in discussing the qualities students need to obtain a job, offers a somewhat more realistic picture: "To get a job [students] should be long enough on family connections, long enough on ability or long enough on personality, or a combination of these. Something called acceptability is made up of the sum of its parts. If a man has any of these things, he could get a job. If he has two of them, he can have a choice of jobs; if he has three, he could go anywhere."[72]

As recently as the early 1960s, when I graduated from law school, there was still a double standard, based on religion and ethnicity, for the hiring of lawyers by corporate law firms. My own story is revealing. I graduated from Yale Law School first in my class and was editor in chief of *The Yale Law Journal*. I was on my way to two prestigious law clerkships, including one on the Supreme Court. Yet when I applied for a summer job in a law firm—the route to permanent employment—I was turned down by *all* the Wall Street and white-shoe firms to which I applied. Most didn't even give me an interview, and those that did made excuses for not hiring me. Nor was my experience unusual. Nearly all my Jewish classmates—

with the exception of some German Jews with family connections—were turned down. Most of my WASP classmates, even those with substantially lower grades, received offers from the same firms. My Jewish classmates and I were offered jobs at "Jewish" or the very few "mixed" law firms (the "mixed" firms were in reality "Jewish" firms with a few token WASPs in visible roles), though even at those firms the WASP applicants received preference. Indeed, I was offered a summer job at one of those firms—Paul, Weiss—only to have the offer withdrawn when the senior partner learned that I was an Orthodox Jew who couldn't work on Saturday. That was simply the way it was in those days.

Within a few years, this situation changed considerably, first in New York and Washington and then in other large cities. Today Jewish lawyers—including Orthodox Jews—not only are welcome at the most distinguished Wall Street law firms but have assumed leadership positions at many of them. But even when discrimination was at its worst, some Jewish lawyers managed to reach the top ranks of the profession, though generally in specified areas that were regarded as "suitable" for their particular "talents." Among these areas were real estate law, litigation, and corporate proxy battles.

Malcolm Gladwell, in his best-selling book *Outliers*, tells the story of Joe Flom, who grew up in my Brooklyn neighborhood of Boro Park a generation before me and graduated from City College and Harvard Law School.[73] Like others of our time, he was turned down by the major Wall Street law firms and went to work for a small "start-up" law firm, where he developed a niche practice that the WASP firms disdained as "ungentlemanly"—aggressive corporate takeovers. He quickly became the go-to lawyer for takeover cases, which rapidly increased in frequency during the 1970s and 1980s. Before long, he was the head of a two-thousand-person law firm—Skadden, Arps, Slate, Meagher & Flom—that was outpacing the traditional firms in virtually every measure of success. Here is how Gladwell describes what Flom achieved:

> Today Skadden, Arps has nearly two thousand attorneys in twenty-three offices around the world and earns well over $1 billion a year,

making it one of the largest and most powerful law firms in the world. In his office, Flom has pictures of himself with George Bush Sr. and Bill Clinton. He lives in a sprawling apartment in a luxurious building on Manhattan's Upper East Side. For a period of almost thirty years, if you were a Fortune 500 company about to be taken over or trying to take over someone else, or merely a big shot in some kind of fix, Joseph Flom has been your attorney and Skadden, Arps has been your law firm—and if they weren't, you probably wished they were.[74]

Gladwell argues that the remarkable success of Jewish lawyers like Flom—who died in 2011 at age eighty-seven—was attributable in part to their status as "outliers": "that he was Jewish at a time when Jews were heavily discriminated against; that he grew up in the Depression—turn out, unexpectedly, to have been advantageous."[75]

But what might have been an advantage for Joe Flom was certainly a disadvantage for many of his co-religionists, who didn't have his skills, determination, and luck! For the average Jewish lawyer, discrimination was a distinct disadvantage, especially in competition with the average non-Jewish lawyer. Only the exceptional Jewish lawyer, like Flom or Arthur Liman or Martin Lipton, could turn general disadvantage into individualized advantage by exploiting the niche left by the discriminating law firms. I don't believe that the Gladwell "outlier" thesis fully explains the disproportionate success of Jewish lawyers in nearly every aspect of the law, ranging from law firm practice, to legal academia, to judging, to public interest law, and even to legal writing.[76]

Nor do I believe that any singular explanation will emerge. The one that perhaps is closest is the broadest: Jewish culture throughout the ages. I will elaborate on this theme in the epilogue of this book, which is about the future of Jewish lawyers.

# EPILOGUE

## The Future of Abraham's Descendants

Having gazed in retrospect at the different categories of Jewish lawyers throughout history—from idol shatterers, to human rights
advocates, to "house Jews," to law teachers, to advisers of those in power,
to collaborators in evil, to successful commercial lawyers—we are now
in a better position to peer into the future. Jewish lawyers and lawgivers,
from Abraham, to Moses, to Louis Brandeis, to Elena Kagan, have had a
profound influence on the rule of law. I end this exploration of the role of
Jewish lawyers by asking the following question: In light of the expected
diminution of Jews in many parts of the world, at least as a percentage of
the population, will the number and influence of Jewish lawyers diminish
in the coming generations? Put another way, will God's prophecy regarding the number of Abraham's descendants—Jews in general and Jewish
lawyers like Abraham in particular—be fulfilled?

In order to assess the relationship between quantity and influence, we
must first ask a question that is asked so often, sometimes with a positive
and other times a negative implication: Why are there so many Jewish
lawyers? Why not? Do you have a problem with that? Jews are quarrel-
some people. Even God called us stiff-necked. We argue with everybody.
And why shouldn't we, considering our heritage? In Genesis 17, God
selects Abraham to become the father of his people, and by Genesis 18
Abraham is already arguing with God over God's plan to destroy Sodom.

Our Torah commands us to pursue justice ("Justice, justice shall
thou *pursue*")[1] and not to stand idly by the blood of our neighbor.[2] Our
Talmud is the first religious compendium to preserve a record of legal

arguments—with dissenting and concurring opinions. We fought against persecution, discrimination, and victimization for millennia. Our rabbis have served as advocates, judges, and lawmakers, resolving disputes among quarreling Jews for centuries. Even our jokes reflect our contentiousness, as in the one about the Jew who was finally rescued from a desert island after ten years of solitude. The rescuers notice that he has built two synagogues. When they ask why, he replies, "That one I pray in; the other one I don't get along with." A variation on that theme has an Israeli on the island with five newspapers: "This one I read; the others I wrap my garbage in."

The opposite side of the contentious image is reflected by the joke involving the rabbi who was presiding over a matrimonial dispute. After the wife finishes complaining about her abusive and philandering husband, the rabbi solemnly declares, "My daughter, you are right." The husband then presents his case against his lazy and shrewish wife, to which the rabbi responds, "My son, you are right." The rabbi's student interjects: "But, Rabbi, they can't both be right." The rabbi pauses and says, "My student, you are right."[3]

In light of this long tradition of contentiousness—coupled with an equally long tradition of mediating disputes and counseling those in power, which began with Joseph—it is not surprising that today's Jews, who constitute less than 2 percent of the population of the United States and a fraction of a percent worldwide, have become a dominant force in the legal profession, both in this country and throughout Europe, South America, Canada, Australia, South Africa, and everywhere else Jews live.

This was not always the case back in the first quarter of the twentieth century, when Jews began to attend law school in significant numbers and the established bar tried desperately to keep Jews from becoming lawyers. The elite of the bar—ranging from Chief Justice William Howard Taft and the Columbia Law School dean Harlan F. Stone, to the American Bar Association president Elihu Root, to the dean of the legal ethics bar, Henry S. Drinker—had no difficulty defining a Jewish lawyer, because there was little intermarriage or assimilation. These bigots knew one when they saw one. Stone described us as exhibiting "racial tendencies toward study by memorization" and "a mind almost Oriental in its fidelity to the minutiae of the subject without regard to any controlling rule or reason"—an absurd, and totally false, racist caricature.[4] Drinker characterized us as "Russian Jew boys" who came "up out of the gutter [and] were merely following the methods [our] fathers had been using in selling shoe-strings and other merchandise."[5] This from the lawyer who lectured other lawyers about "ethics." Others wrote of "Jewey" attitudes and Jewish "acquisitive tendencies." James Beck, a former solicitor general of the United States, urged collective action to keep Jews out of the practice of law: "If the old American stock can be organized, we can still avert the threatened decay of constitutionalism in the country."[6]

And organize they did. According to Jerold S. Auerbach's book *Unequal Justice*, local bar associations conducted discriminatory "character" exams, designed for the explicit purpose of keeping Jews and other undesirables out of the legal profession. When it was proposed that objective higher educational standards be used instead of subjective character tests, one leading bar association lawyer objected on the ground that higher educational requirements might "keep our own possibly out."[7] And these bigoted character committees succeeded, at least in the short run. The number of Jews excluded from the legal profession rose considerably during the late 1920s and early 1930s as more and more Jews failed "character" tests designed to keep them in their fathers' shoestring businesses rather than in the practice of law.

Many law schools cooperated as well, setting Jewish quotas, accepting the established practices of the elite law firms in refusing to hire Jewish graduates, and steering their own Jewish graduates to the Jewish law firms that had emerged in response to this discrimination. For purposes of preserving this apartheid approach to the practice of law, it didn't much matter whether Professor Sanford Levinson's fictional "Jonathan Goldberg" had a non-Jewish mother or went to synagogue. He was a "Jew boy" as far as the elite law firms were concerned.

To be certain that "closeted" Jews didn't slip through the cracks by shortening their names and/or noses, "restricted" or discriminatory institutions required photographs, mother's maiden name, and other tell-tale indicia of Jewishness. This led to the joke about a man with a thick Jewish accent applying to change his name to O'Reilly. When the judge asked him what his current name was, he replied, "O'Brien. I changed it yesterday from Shmulevitz." The judge wondered, "Why are you changing it again?" to which the Jewish man replied, "So ven dey esk me vaht my name used to be, I can tell dem O'Brien."

By the mid-1960s—shortly after I graduated from law school—the barriers against Jewish lawyers had crumbled, and by the 1980s Jewish men had become members of most of the major law firms that had previously restricted them. Jews had moved from pariahs to partners in one generation and then to managing partners in less than another.[8]

The situation was different for Jewish women, as it was for all women. Like Ruth Bader Ginsburg, women who graduated at the top of their classes could not get jobs in many elite law firms, law schools, or corporations. Discrimination against women remained rampant even as Jewish men became partners, professors, and CEOs.

By the 1970s and 1980s, things began to improve as more women went to law school and distinguished themselves. But past discriminatory practices are reflected in the small number of women who are included in my list of great lawyers, Jewish or non-Jewish, *from the past*. Any *future* list of prominent Jewish lawyers will include large numbers of women, including Justice Elena Kagan, former dean of the Harvard Law School; Professor Susan Estrich, the first woman president of the *Harvard Law Review*; Martha Minow, the current dean of the Harvard Law School; Justice Dorit Beinisch, the first woman chief justice of Israel; Justice Rosalie Abella of the Canadian Supreme Court; Minister Tzipi Livni, who has served in several Israeli cabinet posts, including minister of justice; Elizabeth Holtzman, former district attorney of Brooklyn; Jamie Gorelick, former deputy attorney general of the United States; Lydia Kess, an Orthodox woman who in 1971 became the first female partner at the elite white-shoe firm Davis Polk & Wardwell;[9] and many other Jewish women who are just beginning what promise to be distinguished careers in the law.

Glass ceilings still remain, as does discrimination against other groups, such as Asian Americans. Without trying to count the numbers with any precision, we can fairly say that there are more Jews—both men and women—in proportion to their numbers in the general population, in positions of power in the legal profession than any other ethnic or religious group. The same is true of judges, law professors, and deans of law schools.

In light of the history of Jewish victimization, it is not surprising that Jewish lawyers have long been among the leaders in the civil rights movement, the quest for international human rights, the feminist movement, gay rights, environmental protection, and the provision of legal services to indigents. But Jews are also active in conservative legal causes, such as the Federalist Society. Even the chief counsel for Pat Robertson's American Center for Law and Justice was born Jewish, though he now practices Christianity. Every list of the most influential lawyers in the United States is dominated by Jewish names. It is difficult to imagine today's legal profession without Jews. We have become the legal establishment while also remaining its dissidents. (It was also difficult to imagine the legal profession of Weimar Germany without Jews, but . . .)

But as quickly as Jewish lawyers moved from second- to first-class status in the legal profession, we may vanish altogether from the American legal scene and from the legal scenes of other countries with diminishing Jewish populations. This is because American Jews as a whole—at least those kinds of American Jews who become lawyers—are beginning a decline that may bring a virtual end to any significant presence of non-Orthodox Jews in the country by the middle of this century.[10]

The statistics are daunting. We were nearly 4 percent of the U.S. population in 1937. We are below 2 percent today and shrinking. Although many non-Jews believe that Jews constitute 20 percent of the American population—because of our high visibility in the media, the professions, and business—we are, in fact, a tiny and dwindling minority. We have lower birthrates, higher intermarriage rates, and a higher level of assimilation than ever before. This is because, as individuals, Jews have greater opportunities than ever—to marry members of any other group, to work and live in traditionally gentile areas, and to choose how many children not to have (a freedom denied, at least in theory, to some ultra-Orthodox Jews).

Jewish lawyers are in the vanguard of these trends, because they are among the wealthiest, most acculturated, best educated, most successful, and least religious of Jews—precisely those kinds of Jews who are most quickly dwindling in numbers. To be sure, there are Orthodox Jews— some quite distinguished—in the legal profession. Now even some extremely Orthodox Jews who did not attend traditional colleges are being admitted to elite law schools and achieving remarkable academic records. But the vast majority of Jewish lawyers are not particularly observant, and almost none are Hasidic Jews, whose birthrate is above average and whose intermarriage and assimilation rates are negligible.

A chart prepared by Antony Gordon and Richard Horowitz projects four generations into the future and, employing current rates of child-bearing and intermarriage, demonstrates that two hundred secular Jews (a category into which many Jewish lawyers fit) will produce only ten future Jews, while two hundred Hasidic Jews (a category into which hardly any Jewish lawyers fit because Hasidim do not generally attend college, although recently some have been admitted to law schools) will produce more than five thousand future Jews. If these projections are any-where close to accurate, there will be plenty of Hasidic Jews but hardly any Jewish lawyers by the time we celebrate our tercentennial in 2076. These projected trends seem exaggerated to some demographers, but even more recent and more conservative projections suggest a consider-able reduction in American Jewish lawyers by the end of this century.[11]

There will, of course, be many lawyers who will be partially Jewish by heritage. But most of them will not be Jews by religion or by membership in the Jewish community. This is likely because current demographic data show that the vast majority of children and grandchildren of mixed mar-riages are not raised exclusively as Jews and do not identify themselves as Jewish in conventional ways.[12] Nor is there much that can be done to reverse these trends, because the primary cause of the reduction in the number of Jews is the great success Jews are currently experiencing.

When I was a youngster, nobody wanted to marry a Jew. Today everyone wants to marry a Jew—except, apparently, other Jews. When I was a young lawyer, Jewish lawyers practiced law primarily with other Jewish lawyers. Today the practice of law is far more integrated, as are schools, neighborhoods, summer camps, and other places where people meet and marry. When Jews were persecuted, discriminated against, and marginalized, they tended to circle the wagons and stick together. Today Jews live in what I call "the post-persecution era of Jewish history"—at least in America. We do not feel the need for religious or ethnic cohesiveness as much as we did when we were ostracized. Jews who are strongly and publicly pro-Israel may feel the need for cohesiveness, especially on university campuses that are hostile to Israel and its supporters, but much of this hostility comes from other Jews who are anti-Israel.

Today's Jewish lawyers live among non-Jews, go to school with non-Jews, work with non-Jews, and, not surprisingly, often marry non-Jews and raise their children and grandchildren as assimilated Americans. Jews have been welcomed into the most prominent of American families, including the Roosevelts, the Kennedys, the Clintons, the Bidens, the Cuomos, and the Rockefellers. The primary cause of our assimilation today is not hate, as it was in prior generations, but rather love. And it is difficult and futile to fight against love.

The bottom line, therefore, is that the number and percentage of Jewish lawyers practicing, teaching, and judging by the second half of this century will be considerably lower than the number and percentage now. There will, of course, be more "half-Jewish" lawyers, despite the halachic rule that a person born to a Jewish mother and a non-Jewish father is *fully Jewish* and a person born to a Jewish father and a non-Jewish mother is *fully non-Jewish*. In American Jewish jargon, however, the term "half-Jewish" has come to be used in a pragmatic if self-serving way. If someone born to a Jewish father and a non-Jewish mother does something commendable, such as winning a Nobel Prize, we claim him, as in "Do you know that he's half-*Jewish*!" But if someone born to a Jewish mother and a non-Jewish father does something shameful, we disclaim him, as in "You know he's only *half*-Jewish." (Jews are also good in linguistics.) This phenomenon raises the intriguing question of whether the nature of law practice in America will change along with this dramatic demographic change.

There can be little doubt that the influx of Jews into the legal mainstream over the past half century has changed the nature of law practice. Competition increased, the practice became less conservative, and the integration of other excluded groups—women, African Americans, Hispanics, people who are openly gay—moved more quickly once Jews entered the profession. In one sense, the bigoted former solicitor general James Beck was right. When "old American stock" dominated the legal profession, the practice of law was different from when Jews began to enter in large numbers. I think the changes, for the most part, have been positive. I doubt he would agree.

Some critics argue that law has become more of a "business" and less of a "learned profession" since the days of legal apartheid. And, indeed, it was Steven Brill—a Jewish lawyer—who brought the business aspect of law practice to the surface with the 1979 debut of his publication *The American Lawyer*. I believe even these changes have been largely for the better because they have made things more honest. After all, the practice of law is a business as well as a profession. In any event, there can be little doubt that the Jewish influence on the practice of law in this country over the past several decades has been considerable, in part by making it more inclusive and in part by making it more profitable (at least at the top of the profession).

It does not follow, of course, that the diminution in the number and percentage of Jewish lawyers during the remainder of this century will have a comparable impact. That will depend on the answers to several complex questions.

First, is there a uniquely Jewish way of being a lawyer? In his essay "Identifying the Jewish Lawyer," Sanford Levinson makes an intriguing analogy between law and baseball. He asks whether Sandy Koufax was a "Jewish ballplayer." It is true, of course, that the great Brooklyn (and, to my everlasting regret, Los Angeles) Dodger refused to pitch on Yom

Kippur, even during the World Series. This made him a Jewish hero. (I can certainly attest to that, because he and his parents lived a block away from me during his early baseball career.) Levinson says,

> It is crucial to recognize the limited nature of Koufax's status as a Jewish pitcher. That identity comes from his refusal to pitch on Yom Kippur. Yet what about those days he did pitch? Could anyone looking at his behavior as a pitcher—the choice of pitches, his particular pitching "style"—argue that this had anything to do with his being Jewish? . . .
>
> All we can say with confidence is that Koufax's Jewishness, on occasion, would dictate when he would engage in his role as a professional baseball player, just as a Jewish physicist might not perform experiments on Yom Kippur, but not how that role would be performed. One would not expect an analyst to describe the physicist as "performing experiments like a Jew" or to say that Koufax "pitched like a Jew."[13]

(The Nazis did, of course, condemn "Jewish physics.") The former Harvard president Charles Eliot might have begged to differ. When he learned that one Harvard pitcher threw curveballs, he immediately objected to the sport on the following ground: "I understand that a curveball is thrown with a deliberate attempt to deceive. Surely this is not an ability we should want to foster at Harvard."[14] Koufax raised deception to a high art with his four-seam fastball and his overhand curve, though there is no evidence that his deceptive approach derived from his Jewish background, just as there is no evidence that there is anything uniquely Jewish about lawyers who practice lawful deception to win their cases. (Unless they learned it from Abraham's deceptions in describing Sarah as his sister!)

Being a lawyer is, of course, different from being a pitcher or even a physicist. For me, my Jewish heritage greatly influences my life. I think Jewishly. I teach and practice law Jewishly. I conduct my professional and personal life Jewishly. My family life is Jewish, and my politics are Jewishly inspired. Even my agnosticism is Jewish, because the God whose existence I wonder about is the Jewish God.

When I confront a personal or professional problem, I consult Jewish sources as well as American and universal sources. I do not feel compelled to obey the Jewish answers, but I consult the Jewish sources because I value their wisdom. They provide a worldview that reflects an ancient tradition of which I am a part. My Jewish views help me challenge conventional wisdom, just as modern learning enables me to challenge traditional Jewish views. To ignore the wisdom of our sages is both arrogant and ignorant. It would be like deciding a complex constitutional issue without bothering to find out what the framers of our Constitution had in mind.

Just as there is no one way of being a Jew, there is no one way of practicing law Jewishly. But just as there is a common core of being a Jew, there is a common core of being a Jewish lawyer. The bigots of the bar thought they knew what it meant to be a Jewish lawyer back in the 1920s. They associated Jewish lawyers with greed, aggressiveness, and shoddy ethics. In fact, Jewish lawyers have been involved disproportionately in pro bono representation, cause-oriented litigation, government service, human rights and civil rights work, constitutional protection, and other public interest activities. Among the concepts that have characterized many Jewish lawyers have been "Thou shall not stand idly by,"[15] "Do not place a stumbling block in front of the blind,"[16] "Repair the world,"[17] "Have compassion for the downtrodden,"[18] and the difficult pursuit of justice.[19] Several years ago, *The New York Times Magazine* had an article about John Rosenberg, a Jewish immigrant from Nazi Germany who made his life in the most un-Jewish of places, rural Kentucky—trying to bring justice to the poor. Among his associates were three other lawyers with Jewish-sounding names (David Rubinstein, Dan Goldberg, and Ira Newman). Although the title of the piece, "What's a Nice Jewish Lawyer like John Rosenberg Doing in Appalachia?," tried to make it seem unusual, it is not. Because whenever the downtrodden need legal representation, you will often find a Jewish lawyer refusing to stand idly by, repairing the world, showing compassion, and seeking justice.

This does not mean, of course, that non-Jews cannot arrive at the same point by consulting Christian or other sources or that Jews make better lawyers than non-Jews. It does suggest that we are all the products of our experiences, personal and historical, and that these experiences may inform the manner in which we practice our professions and live our lives. I know that I chose to become a criminal defense lawyer at least in part because I am Jewish. I was taught from the earliest age that Jews must always remember that they were persecuted and that we must stand up for those who now face persecution. "Thou shall not stand idly by the blood of thy neighbor" was more than a slogan. "Repair the world" was an imperative. I recall vividly a class in Talmud in which I learned that a Jewish Sanhedrin (religious court) that had imposed the death penalty by a unanimous vote in one day could not carry out the sentence, because unanimity and haste suggested that the accused might not have had a zealous advocate presenting his arguments within the tribunal.[20] I also learned that the youngest judge in the Sanhedrin always spoke first, so that his views would have to be considered. I recall mentioning that to my mentor Justice Arthur Goldberg and my Harvard colleague Justice Stephen Breyer, who, as the junior justices of their respective Supreme Courts, were also told to speak first at conferences of the justices.

I always wanted to be a Jewish lawyer, and though many Jews disapprove of some of my clients, I believe I am a lawyer in the Jewish tradition[21]—a tradition that includes Abraham's zealous representation of the sinners of Sodom. I also believe that many other Jewish lawyers are influenced by their Jewish heritage in the way they practice law, teach law, or judge. (I recently described a great federal judge in Boston, who is Jewish, as "a mensch on the bench.")[22] So the dwindling of Jewish lawyers during this century may well have a profound impact on the general practice of law in America and other places and on the social conscience of the law in particular.

But it is also possible that the Jewish influence on the law has become so pervasive that it will continue even in the absence of large numbers of Jewish lawyers. For example, if Jews were to vanish from the face of the earth—as we almost did during the Holocaust—the influences of the Jewish Bible would continue because much of the non-Jewish world has incorporated the Jewish Bible into their own religions and worldviews. Would the same be true of the influence of Jewish lawyers? I believe it might, for several interesting reasons. First and foremost, the influence of Jewish lawyers—and of the Jewish tradition of law—has become an important part of the American legal system. The privilege against self-incrimination, the idea that it is better that ten guilty go free than one innocent be confined, the concept of equal protection for all, and the notion of proportionality between a crime and its punishment all have roots in Jewish law. Even the controversial concept of affirmative action has a basis in Jewish tradition, as evidenced by the story of the rabbi who was asked whether a congregant who was wealthy and contributed more to the synagogue should have a greater vote on the policies of the synagogue. The rabbi replied, "You are right about a congregant's wealth determining his vote, but you are wrong about your conclusion: the poor should have a greater vote, because the wealthy already have too much influence on synagogue policy by virtue of their wealth."[23] Without the continuing presence of Jewish lawyers to nurture this influence, it is still likely to continue, though perhaps with less recognition of its Jewish heritage.

Moreover, there will still be many lawyers—indeed, even more than there are today—who reflect a partial Jewish heritage. There is every reason to believe that lawyers of partial Jewish heritage will continue to practice law in a somewhat Jewish manner, even as they go to synagogues less often or identify less with an exclusively Jewish heritage. The great paradox of American Jewish life is that most of the positive values we identify with Jews—compassion, creativity, contributions to the world at large, charity, a quest for a broad education—seem more characteristic of secular or moderately religious Jews than of ultra-Orthodox Jews. There are exceptions, of course, but it seems the closer one lives to the religious core of Judaism, the further one is likely to be from many of the Jewish values so many of us cherish.[24]

However, it is possible that even if the number and percentage of Jews were to increase in this century—an extremely unlikely prospect in light of the current demographics—their unique influence would still diminish. This would be so if their past influence were exclusively a result of their history of persecution and poverty and the progressive values that stem from such a background. Tomorrow's Jewish lawyers, who are children and grandchildren of the high, mighty, and wealthy, might act like other children and grandchildren of the high, mighty, and wealthy. Experience does not suggest that this will happen, though. One sociologist quipped that Jews live like Episcopalians but vote like Puerto Ricans.[25] Although Jews have never been the direct beneficiaries of affirmative action—indeed, many have been disadvantaged by it—a significant majority of Jewish Californians voted to preserve race-based affirmative action programs, apparently because they thought it was the right thing.[26]

The Talmud teaches that since the destruction of the Second Temple in Jerusalem (about seventy years after the birth of Jesus), prophecy has been limited to fools.[27] It is impossible to assess accurately the impact that the diminishing Jewish population will have on American life in general or on the law in particular. The bagel will endure, along with the many colorful words—from "schlep" to "schmuck" to "yenta" to "chutzpah"—we have contributed to the American lexicon. Jewish jokes will continue, even in the absence of as many Jewish comedians to tell them. I hope that the Jewish legacy in law will persist as well—a legacy that has had so great an impact in so short a period of time. But there are no guarantees. An America without Jews will be a less exciting, innovative, progressive, compassionate place. (Just as an America without blacks, Hispanics, gays, women, Asians, Greeks, Irish, Italians, and—hard as it is to imagine—WASPs would be a less interesting place.)

The Jewish contribution has never been a matter of quantity. Even so, if our numbers and percentage are so reduced that we fall below the 1 percent mark, which is likely to occur in the not-too-distant future, our influence will necessarily become marginalized.

It may be difficult to remember the days during the first part of the twentieth century when there were more Jewish athletes and gangsters than lawyers and journalists. Now, instead of playing on basketball teams, we own them; instead of boxing in rings, we own the casinos in which the matches are held; and instead of belonging to Murder Incorporated, we represent those accused of murder and mayhem. As Ecclesiastes said, "To everything there is a season."[28] Perhaps we will soon witness the end of the Jewish season in the American courtroom and law firm. We will have left our mark, as Abraham—our first lawyer—left his mark on us. We will continue to leave a mark, but we will be different, and the mark we leave will be different. That has always been the nature of Jewish life, wherever we have lived. But just as an America with far fewer Jews will be a less creative and compassionate place, an American legal profession with far fewer Jewish lawyers will be a less creative and compassionate profession.

Just as Abraham changed over time—from a radical idol shatterer, to a zealous but polite advocate, to a rescuer of prisoners, to a compliant accepter of an immoral command, to an affluent real estate lawyer—so too have his successors changed and will continue to change as both Jewish life and the legal profession change.

# ACKNOWLEDGMENTS

The Jewish tradition of commentating on texts enriches the learning experience. In that tradition, this book has been enriched most especially by the comments and contributions of Elliot Schwab, who did an excellent job researching traditional and other Jewish sources, and of Hila Solomon, who did an excellent job researching Christian and Muslim sources. My appreciation goes as well to Sarah Neely, Rabbi William Hamilton, Rabbi Lauren Berkun, Alan Rothfeld, Sarah Miller, and Carolyn Cohen for their insights and assistance.

# NOTES

## Introduction: The Jewish Lawyer

1. See Genesis 41.
2. See Exodus 32:33; see also pp. 27–8, *supra*.
3. See ch. 2, n. 4, *infra*.
4. Judges 4:5.
5. But see John Noble Wilford, "Camels Had No Business in Genesis," *New York Times*, Feb. 10, 2014, Science sec. According to Genesis 24, Abraham and his servants "took 10 camels" and journeyed to another city. But according to historians, camels were not domesticated until many centuries after the patriarchs were supposed to have lived. See ibid.
6. But see Jon D. Levenson, *Inheriting Abraham: The Legacy of the Patriarch in Judaism, Christianity, and Islam* (Princeton, N.J.: Princeton University Press, 2012), 12.
7. Although the Qur'an states that Abraham is neither a Jew nor a Christian, it recognizes that he is the first monotheist. Roberto Tottoli, *Biblical Prophets in the Qur'an and Muslim Literature* (Oxford, U.K.: Routledge, 2002), 26. The Muslim commentator Ibn Mardaweh explains, "Abraham is the most noble following the Prophet Muhammad." Brannon M. Wheeler, *Prophets in the Quran: An Introduction to the Quran and Muslim Exegesis* (New York: Continuum, 2002), 107. Indeed, Abraham, apart from Moses, is mentioned more than any other figure in the Qur'an. Hans-Josef Klauck et al., *Encyclopedia of the Bible and Its Reception* (New York: Walter de Gruyter, 2009), 189.
8. In Judaism, Midrash is the collection of rabbinic homiletic anecdotes, legends, and commentaries on the Tanach (Jewish Bible or Old Testament). References throughout this book to "the Midrash" generally refer to Genesis Rabbah, the most popular midrashic work on Genesis, which was written and organized during the early medieval period.
9. "How dare you" is my interpretative translation. For others, see p. 15 and n. 14, *infra*.
10. Babylonian Talmud, Sanhedrin 105a.
11. See Mishnah, Avot 1:14.
12. A recent example is the absurd charge that the only reason Israel grants equality to gays is to "pink wash" Israel's bad treatment of Palestinians.
13. Some of these "fences" seem more like prison bars, such as the recent prohibition issued by some ultra-Orthodox rabbis against smart phones, because one can access "bad" things on such phones.

14. Shalom Spiegel, *The Last Trial*, trans. Judah Goldin (New York: Pantheon, 1967).

15. See Hannah Arendt, *Eichmann in Jerusalem* (New York: Penguin, 2006).

16. See Daniel Maier-Katkin and Birgit Maier-Katkin, "Love and Reconciliation: The Case of Hannah Arendt and Martin Heidegger," *Harvard Review* 32 (2007): 34–48.

17. I had the privilege of representing some of them, including Anatoly Sharansky.

18. I have been privileged to defend Israel in many of these confrontations and have been called Israel's "lead attorney in the court of public opinion." See "Forward 50 2007," *Jewish Daily Forward*, http://forward.com/forward-50-2007/.

19. See my discussion of Judah Benjamin, Louis Brandeis, and Joseph Flom, pp. 93–5, 113–15, 124–5, *supra*.

## Part I.   The Biblical Narrative: The Lawyer Abraham

### 1.  God Meets Abram—and So Do We

1. According to Islamic legend, Abraham's mother's pregnancy was hidden from King Nimrod, who had ordered his soldiers to kill all male babies. Jan Knappert, *Islamic Legends: Histories of the Heroes, Saints and Prophets of Islam* (Leiden, Netherlands: E. J. Brill, 1985), 1:72–73. This legend is reminiscent of the biblical story of baby Moses's mother hiding him from Pharaoh, who had decreed that all male babies be cast in the Nile. Exodus 2:1. The baby Moses story also appears in the Qur'an, at 28:3–8.

2. The Midrash relies on a subtle textual hint to support this prequel. Namely, the verse in Genesis (11:28) states, "And Haran died *on the face of* his father Terah" (the italicized phrase is translated literally from the original Hebrew). This phrase is typically understood to mean Haran died during Terah's lifetime, but the Midrash notes that even according to that interpretation the relevance of this fact is unclear. The Midrash thus posits that Haran died "*on account of*" his father, Terah, and it proceeds to tell a story beginning with the idol altercation and ending with Haran's death. Genesis Rabbah 38:11.

3. An intriguing essay by Nathaniel Helfgot claims that the midrashic rabbis might have extrapolated the Abram-idol story from a similar story relating to Gideon the judge in Judges 6:25–32, wherein the young Gideon destroys his father's altar to the false god Ba'al. When Gideon faces death for his blasphemy, his father defends him, arguing that if Ba'al is a true god, "let him fight his own battles, since it is his own altar that has been destroyed." Nathaniel Helfgot, *Mikra and Meaning* (New Milford, Conn.: Maggid Books, 2012), 55–64.

4. I number the commandments in accord with the Jewish tradition.

5. Although neither the Ten Commandments nor the Torah was yet in existence, some rabbis cited in the Talmud insist that the patriarchs knew and obeyed them. Babylonian Talmud, Yoma 28b. In the context of Abraham's abandoning his father en route to the promised land, some commentators contend that Abra-

ham did not "invoke the Fifth" because he was not required to honor his father, either because Terah was an idolater or because Abraham was considered a convert and therefore lacked a halachic father. See, for example, Rashi, Genesis 11:32; *Sefer HaMakneh* (eighteenth century) in his commentary on Babylonian Talmud, Kiddushin 31b.

6.  There are several rabbinic versions of the idol story. The most frequently cited is from Genesis Rabbah 38:11:

> Terah leaves on a trip and puts his son in charge of the shop. A woman comes in with a plate of fine flour and leaves it with the request that Abram offer it to the gods. Instead, he takes a club and smashes all the idols but the largest, in the hand of which he then leaves the club:
>
> > When his father came back, he said, "What have you done to them!" He replied, "Why should I hide it from you? A woman came with a plate of fine flour and asked me to offer it to them. One said, 'I'm eating it first!' and another one said, 'I'm eating it first!' The biggest one then took the club and smashed them." He said, "Why are you deceiving me? Do they know anything?" He answered, "Do your ears not hear what is coming out of your mouth?"
>
> Unable to refute his son's argument, Terah turns Abram over to the idolatrous King Nimrod, and Nimrod, a fire-worshipper, consigns him to the flames (*'ur*). Yet Abram emerges unscathed. (Levenson, *Inheriting Abraham,* 119)

7.  Genesis Rabbah 38:11. The Qur'an too tells the story of Abraham the idol smasher, though a bit differently from the Jewish sources from which it was drawn:

> And we gave Abraham his right judgment formerly; for We knew him well. When he said to his father and his people: "What are those statues to which you are devoted?" They said: "We found our fathers worshipping them." He said: "Indeed, you and your fathers have been in manifest error." They said: "Have you brought us the truth, or are you one of those who jest?" He said: "No, your Lord is the Lord of the heavens and the earth, Who created them both; and I bear witness to that. And by Allah, I will show your idols my guile, after you turn your backs."
> Then he reduced them to pieces except for their chief, so that they might turn to him. When the people then ask Abraham whether he committed the crime, he has his answer ready: "No, but their chief did this; so ask them if they can speak." In the end, the idolaters "were utterly confounded," and the iconoclast draws the familiar conclusion: "He [Abraham] said: 'Do you, then, worship, besides Allah, what does not profit or harm you a whit?'" (Qur'an 21:51–66, quoted in Levenson, *Inheriting Abraham,* 121)

According to Islamic legend, "The priests and elders of the people were then mentally and intellectually confounded by the logic of the young teenager who stood confronting them. The accusers had become the accused, i.e., accused of illogic and intellectual inconsistency, and they did not know how to answer." Jerald F. Dirks, *Abraham the Friend of God* (Beltsville, Md.: Amana, 2002), 39. This is reminiscent of the way Jesus is portrayed in the New Testament, defeating Pharisees in logical arguments. Islamic commentator Robert Tottoli comments that Abraham felt relieved of all responsibility "when it became clear . . . that his father was an enemy of God." Tottoli, *Biblical Prophets in the Qur'an and Muslim Literature*, 25.

8. See my discussion of the Akedah, pp. 29–52, *supra*.

9. Exodus 14:11.

10. *The Hirsch Chumash*, trans. Daniel Haberman (Nanuet, N.Y.: Feldheim, 2005), II:228.

11. Henry Sumner Maine, *Ancient Law* (London, U.K.: John Murray, 1908), 150–51. "Starting, as from one terminus of history, from a condition of society in which all the relations of Persons are summed up in the relations of Family, we seem to have steadily moved towards a phase of social order in which all these relations arise from the free agreement of Individuals. . . . [W]e may say that the movement of the progressive societies has hitherto been a movement from Status to Contract."

12. See George Gilder, *The Israel Test* (Minneapolis: Richard Vigilante Books, 2009).

13. See Aaron David Miller, *The Much Too Promised Land: America's Elusive Search for Arab-Israeli Peace* (New York: Bantam, 2008).

14. On the very first verse in Genesis, Rashi, the eleventh-century rabbinic commentator, cites the following midrash: "If the nations of the world one day challenge the Jewish people for 'stealing' the land of Israel, the latter can point to the first verse of the Bible, which states that God created all lands; if he created it, he is entitled to grant it to whomever he pleases." For a critique of this Rashi, see Alan Dershowitz, *The Genesis of Justice* (New York: Warner Books, 2000), 217–19.

15. An enforceable contract must contain consideration, or a performance or return promise that is bargained for. Restatement (Second) of Contracts § 71. The Uniform Commercial Code, a benchmark for commercial contracting law, requires that a contract contain "agreement" between the parties, "including conduct by both parties which recognizes the existence of such contract." Uniform Commercial Code § 2-204. It also requires that something of "value" be exchanged to warrant "consideration sufficient to support a simple contract." Uniform Commercial Code § 3-303. Contract law provides protection for a promisee who reasonably relied on a promise and took action while relying on that promise—the concept known as "detrimental reliance." Restatement (Second) of Contracts § 90 (1981).

16. See Genesis 15:17.

17. Mark Sheridan, ed., *Genesis 12–50*, Ancient Christian Commentary on Scripture: Old Testament II (Downers Grove, Ill.: InterVarsity Press, 2002), 39. In Christian theology, "Christ is the *executor* of Abraham's will." See ibid.

18. See Levenson, *Inheriting Abraham*, 38, quoting Nachmanides.

19. See ibid., 39, citing recently uncovered historical evidence pointing to an apparent custom in ancient Mesopotamia by which the brother of a fatherless woman often acts as her legal representative and arranges her marriage in place of her nonliving father. Levenson cites the Assyriologist Barry L. Eichler, who suggests based on this custom that Abram's ploy—which did not anticipate Pharaoh's swift abduction of Sarah—was intended to protect his own life, while leaving Abram with control over his wife's marriage and sexuality. An obvious problem with this theory, however, is that it restores Abram's role as an impediment to predatory men, thus placing his life in danger regardless.

20. See Nahum M. Sarna, *Genesis*, JPS Torah Commentary (Philadelphia: Jewish Publication Society, 1989), 143. While it does not precisely fit this ancient practice, the biblical story of King David, Bathsheba, and Uriah is rooted in a similar concept. After David's illicit affair with the married Bathsheba, he learns that he has impregnated her. He decides to send her husband, Uriah, to the front line of battle so that he is killed and conveniently out of the way, whereupon David swoops in and marries Bathsheba. 2 Samuel 11.

21. The Muslim hadith narrator Abu Hurayrah presents the foregoing story as follows:

> When he came to one of the giant kings, the king was told: "There is a man who has the most beautiful of wives." So the king sent for Abraham and asked him: "Who is this?" He said: "My sister." So Sarah came and he said: "Sarah, there is not, on the face of this earth, a believing man except for me and you. If this one asks you, tell him that you are my sister. Do not make a liar out of me." The king sent for Sarah. (Wheeler, *Prophets in the Quran*, 94)

See also Suzanne Haneef, *A History of the Prophets of Islam Derived from the Quran, Ahadith, and Commentaries* (n.p.: Library of Islam, 2002), 1:284–86.

22. The Midrash tells us that Abram was worried as he was entering Egypt, so he locked Sarai in a box. When a customs officer grew suspicious of the contents of the box, he requested that Abram open it. The land of Egypt was then immediately "irradiated with her [beauty]." Rabbi Dr. Freedman et al., trans. and eds., *Midrash Rabbah*, vol. 1, *Genesis* (London: Soncino Press, 1983), 329. But see Ephraim Oshry, *Responsa from the Holocaust* (New York: Judaica Press, 2001), 193–94, allowing women whom the Nazis forced into prostitution to remain married to their husbands after the war.

23. The Jewish medieval commentator Nachmanides was critical of Abram's decision to deceive Pharaoh. He writes, "Abraham our father unintentionally committed a great sin by bringing his righteous wife to a stumbling-block of sin on account of his fear for his life. He should have trusted that G-d would save him and his wife and all his belongings for G-d surely has the power to help and to save." Ramban (Nachmanides), *Commentary on the Torah: Genesis*, trans. Charles B. Chavel (New York: Shilo, 1971), 173.

See also Benno Jacob, *The First Book of the Bible: Genesis*, ed. and trans. Ernest I. Jacob and Walter Jacob (New York: Ktav, 1974), 89–90.

The fourth-century Christian theologian Didymus the Blind writes that Abraham's lie was "an intelligent compromise with the lustfulness of the Egyptians, being certain that God, who had made him leave his own country, would watch over his marriage." Sheridan, *Genesis 12–50*, 6–8.

In contrast with the early commentators, the medieval Christian commentator Saint Jerome seems less concerned with explaining the reasoning behind Abraham's lie. Rather, he seeks to defend Sarah "by suggesting that she acted under duress, and then to show that possibly she may not have had time to be taken to Pharaoh's bed." *Saint Jerome's Hebrew Questions on Genesis*, trans. C.T.R. Hayward (New York: Oxford University Press, 1995), 149.

See also Claus Westermann, *Genesis 12–36: A Commentary*, trans. John J. Scullion (Minneapolis: Augsburg, 1985), 164.

The modern Christian commentator Gerhard von Rad interprets Abraham's act differently from Westermann. Rad writes that Abraham was "afraid that the beauty of his wife . . . could be his undoing" because "the husband of so beautiful a woman is in far greater danger abroad than her brother would be." Rad interprets that story's abrupt ending—God intervenes on behalf of Sarah, and they are "whisked out of Egypt under military escort"—to be a testament to God's "darkness and mystery." One explanation Rad offers is that the story "extols the beauty of the ancestress and the sagacity of the ancestor who knew how to extricate himself so successfully from so precarious a situation with the help of his God." Gerhard von Rad, *Genesis: A Commentary*, trans. John H. Marks (Philadelphia: Westminster Press, 1972), 168–69.

24. Rashi writes that upon Abraham's arrival at Gerar, he knew that the people there had no "fear of God" because "he was asked about his wife, but he was not asked about his arrangement regarding food and drink." In exploring why Abraham felt the need to explain to Abimelech why, in fact, he believed Sarah was his sister, Rashi writes that "Abraham wanted it known that even in a life-threatening situation, he preferred to save himself by telling the truth rather than by saying something false." *The Torah: With Rashi's Commentary Translated, Annotated, and Elucidated*, ed. Yisrael Isser Zvi Herczeg et al. (Brooklyn: Mesorah, 1995), 213. This seems to be a testament to Abraham's commitment to honesty.

In contrast, Nachmanides interprets Abraham's need to explain to Abimelech why he said what he did in a negative light. To Nachmanides, it matters not whether Sarah was truly Abraham's sister or his wife, "for when they wanted to take her as a wife and he told them, She is my sister, in order to lead them astray, he already committed a sin towards them by bringing upon them a great sin, and it no longer mattered at all whether the thing was true or false!" Ramban (Nachmanides), *Commentary on the Torah: Genesis*, 263–64.

Ibn Ezra offers still a different reason for why Abraham justified his statement to Abimelech. Ibn Ezra believes that "Abraham put Abimelech off with a timely excuse." *Ibn Ezra's Commentary on the Pentateuch: Genesis (Bereshit)*, ed. and trans. H. Norman Strickman and Arthur M. Silver (New York: Menorah, 1988), 213.

The modern Jewish commentator Nahum M. Sarna resorts to the oft-cited idea that Abraham lied because he believed "that the king would have him killed in order to avoid committing adultery," but he insightfully intertwines this reasoning with legal underpinnings by observing that "in a situation where no legal sanction or reward is enforceable, the ultimate restraint on evil . . . is the consciousness of the existence of a higher power." Sarna eloquently summarizes Abraham's problem: in the ancient world, where God's word was the force of law, he came into contact with an effectively lawless society. Therefore, he had no choice but to lie. Sarna, *Genesis*, 36–37.

The early Christian commentators focus more on the concept of virtue as an indirect justification for Abraham's potential lie.

Origen, *Homilies on Genesis and Exodus*, trans. Ronald E. Heine (Washington, D.C.: Catholic University of America Press, 1982), 122–23.

Chrysostom, reflecting on Abraham's justification to Abimelech when asked why he said Sarah was his sister, invites the reader to "see what great pains the good man takes to show that he had not told a lie even in this matter." Sheridan, *Genesis 12–50*, 87.

*Saint Jerome's Hebrew Questions on Genesis*, 173; von Rad, *Genesis*, 227–28.

25. Christian commentators have hypothesized that "Abimelech's insistence that Abraham not 'wrong his name' provides occasion for the observation that spreading slanderous rumors is a way of wronging someone's name." Sheridan, *Genesis 12–50*, 100. Judaism contains laws strictly prohibiting even truthful slander (known in Hebrew as *lashon hora*).

26. Sarna writes, "This excuse undoubtedly reflects a sensitivity to resorting to falsehood, even in self-defense. Still, the statement itself must be factual as well as a tradition of great antiquity. . . . [I]t is inconceivable that a late author would invent a tale ascribing to the patriarch a practice abhorrent to the sexual morality of Israel as it found legal expression in the Torah codes (Lev. 18:9,11; 20:17, Deut. 27:22); otherwise, we are led to the preposterous assumption that an incestuous marriage was a lesser offense than falsehood in the eyes of the biblical Narrator." Sarna, *Genesis*, 143.

The modern commentator Benno Jacob criticizes Abraham's lie to Abimelech. Jacob writes, "Abraham has sinned by using a lie, perhaps a white lie, or by expressing himself ambiguously." Jacob, *First Book of the Bible*, 134.

The modern commentator W. Gunther Plaut offers an alternate explanation— one that lies in the interpretation of the word "sister": "Abraham lived about 1500 B.C.E., when the word 'sister' could have an additional, special meaning . . . a Hurrian could adopt his wife as his sister, thereby giving her special status, for she would be treated as a blood relative of her husband's family." Next, Plaut ponders whether "a man can be judged guilty when he has a choice—but what choices are open to a man who, like Abraham, believes he is faced with mortal danger? What could Abraham have done, given the knowledge of the prospects available to him? The text, as it does so often, merely states the problem, leaving it to the reader to ponder it further." Unlike the text, however, Plaut does not leave us wondering. Plaut believes that because "Jewish teaching has generally held that, even under duress, no man may intentionally kill or commit a sexual crime on an innocent person" and because "both Sarah and Pharaoh were put in jeopardy by Abraham," Nachmanides was correct: Abraham's lie was a sin. W. Gunther Plaut, ed., *The Torah: A Modern Commentary*, trans. Jewish Publication Society (New York: Union of American Hebrew Congregations, 1981), 99–100.

27. See Leviticus 18:9, 11; 20:17; Deuteronomy 27:22. These verses explicitly include half siblings in prohibitions of incest.

28. See, for example, Rashi, Genesis 20:12. Another explanation given is that Sarah was actually Abraham's niece—the daughter of his brother Haran—and his nonliteral reference to her as his "sister" is similar to his later reference to Lot—his nephew—as his brother. Ibid. For another justification, offered by Islamic commentators, see Dirks, *Abraham the Friend of God*, 80.

29. Levenson, *Inheriting Abraham*, 40.

30. Ibid., 38. Another illustration of this theme is the parable in which a shipwrecked sailor repeatedly refuses help from another boat, a helicopter, and other rescuers, insisting, "God will save me!" When he dies and meets his Maker, he asks God, "Why did you not save me?" to which God replies, "Who do you think sent you all those rescuers?!"

31. Genesis Rabbah, quoted in Amos W. Miller, *Abraham: Friend of God* (Middle Village, N.Y.: Jonathan David, 1973), 142.

## 2. God Tests Abraham and Abraham Passes—
## at Least the First Test

1. The biblical God of the Jews is not necessarily as omniscient as the Christian, Muslim, or Talmudic Jewish God. He "regrets" creating humans. After acting on that regret and destroying most of the world with the Flood, He seems to regret that decision as well, promising never to repeat it. He is not sure whether the reports of evildoing in Sodom are accurate. He does not "know" that Abraham fears God until after the binding of Isaac. The extent of God's omniscience is indeed debated among medieval Jewish philosophers. The paradox between God's omniscience and man's free will led Hasdai Crescas—a fourteenth-century philosopher and halachist—to conclude that human free will is heavily limited, while Gersonides, another fourteenth-century rationalist, opted for the opposite extreme, limiting God's omniscience in some regards, including foreknowledge of human acts. See Bernard Martin, *A History of Judaism* (New York: Basic Books, 1974), 2:10, 20–21. Abraham ibn Daud (Maimonides's forerunner) likewise held that God lacks such foreknowledge. Isaac Husik, *A History of Mediaeval Jewish Philosophy* (New York: Macmillan, 1916), 230–31.

2. Mishnah, Avot 1:14.

3. See Rashi, Genesis 18:21.

4. The Apocrypha story of Susanna and the elders, which does not appear in the

Jewish Bible, relates how Daniel saved the life of the falsely accused Susanna by insisting that her two accusers be separated during cross-examination so that they could not coordinate their false account. This rule of separating witnesses— which is actually called "the Rule"—is still employed today. See Sarah Chapman Carter, "Exclusion of Justice," *University of Dayton Law Review* 30, no. 1 (2004): 63.

5. Obadiah Sforno, a sixteenth-century commentator, explains God's rhetorical question "Shall I conceal from Abraham that which I do?" to mean the follow-ing: *I must demonstrate to Abraham that I rule fairly and that the city would indeed be redeemed if it contained a sufficient number of righteous people.* See Sforno, Genesis 18:17; see also Ohr HaChaim, Genesis 18:17.

6. See Alan Dershowitz, *Rights from Wrongs: The Origins of Human Rights in the Expe-rience of Injustice* (New York: Basic Books, 2005).

7. See Alan Dershowitz, *Just Revenge* (New York: Warner Books, 1999).

8. While some commentators maintain that Abraham was merely role-playing (see ch. 3, n. 25, *infra*), Obadiah Sforno, a sixteenth-century commentator, writes explicitly that Abraham *doubted God's judgment.* Sforno, Genesis 18:27.

9. According to one midrash, Abraham approached God with a threefold plan: (1) engage in "war" with God by employing forceful argumentation; (2) appease God (probably referring to the deferential phrases cited in *supra*, p. 15); and (3) pray on behalf of the accused. Genesis Rabbah 49:7.

10. According to a midrash, Abraham challenged God as follows: "In the case of a human judge, an appeal can be made to a higher authority. Shall you, because no appeal can be made from your judgment, not do justice? Because there is no one to veto you, shall you not act justly?" Quoted in Miller, *Abraham*, 116.

11. The Christian tradition has Jesus questioning God as he is crucified: "My God, my God, why have You abandoned me?" But that is a far cry from the words directed to God by Abraham.

12. To be sure, Moses's request during the golden calf episode rivals Abraham's bold confrontation with God. After acknowledging the grievous sin that the Israelites had committed, Moses directs God, "And now if You will but forgive their sin— but if not, erase me now from Your book that You have written." Exodus 32:32. See *supra*, pp. 27–8.

13. A Jew who violates the Sabbath is called a "mechalel shabbat"—a profaner of the Sabbath. See Babylonian Talmud, Chullin 5a; cf. Exodus 31:14.

14. In fact, while most standard, modern translations sugarcoat Abraham's bra-zen challenge, the Talmud defines *chalila* as *chulin*—it would be profane for you. Babylonian Talmud, Avodah Zorah 4a. Even Rashi, the conservative commentator—whom I generally consider "the greatest defense attorney" of God and biblical figures—provides this translation. Interestingly, the only other instance in which the Talmud employs the phrase "it would be profane for you" is in reference to Moses's bold ultimatum (see ch. 2, n. 12, *supra*). Based on the lan-guage, *mecheini* (erase me), the Talmud exegetes that Moses told God "Chulin hu lach"—it would be profane for you (*chulin* is etymologically related to *mecheini*). Babylonian Talmud, Berachot 32a.

15. Genesis 18:27–32.
16. Indeed, one early midrash posits that Abraham harbored doubts about the justice of the Flood, finding it hard to believe that there were no righteous people at the time that were swept along with the rest. The midrash continues that God knew that Abraham harbored these suspicions, and He therefore decided to include Abraham in the judicial process on this occasion to demonstrate to him that no righteous people would be slaughtered. See Midrash Tanchuma, Vayeira 5. See also Sforno and Ohr HaChaim on Genesis 18:17.
17. To be sure, it is unclear even that Lot was righteous. The Midrash posits that God saved Lot only on account of his uncle Abraham's merit. Genesis Rabbah 50:11. See also the modern commentator Yehuda Jacobowitz's discussion of Lot's character flaws. Yehuda Jacobowitz, *MeAvirah DeArah* (Jerusalem: Jacobowitz, 2013), 3–7.
18. But see the medieval rabbinic sources cited in ch. 2, n. 1, *supra*, according to which God has no foreknowledge of people's actions.
19. Rashi claims, based on a close textual reading, that Abraham actually argued in the alternative, as good lawyers often do: (1) You should "forgive [the guilty] for the sake of the innocent"; (2) even if You won't forgive the guilty, at least don't "bring death upon the innocent as well as the guilty." Rashi, Genesis 18:24.
20. But see Alan Dershowitz, "Scalia's Catholic Betrayal," *Daily Beast*, Aug. 18, 2009. I wrote this article in response to a dissenting opinion in which Justice Antonin Scalia wrote,

> This court has *never* held that the Constitution forbids the execution of a convicted defendant who has had a full and fair trial but is later able to convince a habeas court that he is "actually" innocent. Quite to the contrary, we have repeatedly left that question unresolved, while expressing considerable doubt that any claim based on alleged "actual innocence" is constitutionally cognizable. (*In re Davis*, 557 U.S. 952 [2009])

In my response, I challenged Scalia to debate me on whether Catholic doctrine permits the execution of a factually innocent person who has been tried without constitutional flaw but whose innocence is clearly established by new and indisputable evidence. (I noted at the time that although it takes chutzpah to challenge a practicing Catholic on the teachings of his own faith, that is a quality we share.) He did not accept my challenge.

21. Rabbi Samson Raphael Hirsch, the nineteenth-century leader of Orthodox German Jewry, considers this entire anomalous episode an illustration of "the godliness of the voice within us that appeals for justice." Hirsch, *The Hirsch Chumash*, 1:429.
22. Job 38–40. God's pulling rank on Job might have reflected a guilty conscience and an inability to justify what He had done to appease Satan. But see Ramban (commentary to Job 42:10), who speculates based on several textual difficulties that God didn't actually kill Job's children. Instead, He authorized Satan to hide them in the desert and send a messenger (ibid. 1:14) to inform Job that his children had been killed, so as to test him without actually harming the children. I based my novel *Just Revenge* on this "Nachmanidean solution," which I fictionalized into the "Naimonickan solution."

23. One midrash seems to draw the following distinction between the two challenges: whereas Abraham only *cautioned* God (*pre facto*), Job took his audacious
   challenge a step further by explicitly *concluding* (*post facto*) that God had committed such an injustice. See Midrash Tanchuma, Vayeira 5.

24. Rabbi Eleazar criticized Abraham for stopping at ten, contrasting him with
   Moses, who insisted that God spare the sinners who built the golden calf even if
   there were no righteous among them. Zohar, bk. 1, p. 106a.

25. Genesis Rabbah, quoted in Miller, *Abraham*, 118.

26. See Aharon Swersky, *Mimayanot Hanetzach* (Bnei Brak, Israel, 1974), on Genesis
   18:33, citing Rabbi Mordechai Yosef of Izhbitza.

27. Henry Brougham, *Speeches of Henry Lord Brougham* (Edinburgh: Adam and
   Charles Black, 1838), 1:105.

28. See R. Shimon Schwab, *Ma'ayan Beit Hashoeva* (Brooklyn: Mesorah, 1994), 40–41.

29. A variation on this hypothetical involves a pizza delivery boy who delivers to
   a hospital's transplant ward that has a dozen patients who will die if they don't
   receive new kidneys, hearts, and so on. Does anyone believe that the delivery
   boy should be killed and his organs used to save a dozen lives? If not, why is that
   case different from the train case?

30. Fyodor Dostoyevsky, *The Brothers Karamazov* (New York: W. W. Norton, 1976),
   226.

31. See ch. 2, n. 35–36, *infra*.

32. See Maimonides, *Mishneh Torah*, Hilchot Sanhedrin 12:3 (translated from the original Hebrew):

   > How do they admonish the witnesses in capital cases? They say to them,
   > "Perhaps what you say is conjecture or hearsay, or secondhand testimony
   > from a reliable person, or perhaps you are unaware that we will eventu-
   > ally cross-examine you. Know that capital cases are unlike civil cases: in
   > civil cases, a person pays money and is atoned; whereas in capital cases, his
   > blood and the blood of his descendants are his [the witness's] responsibility
   > until the end of the world. . . . One who takes a single life, it is as if he has
   > destroyed the entire world, and one who saves a single life, it is as if he
   > has saved the entire world."

   Elsewhere, Maimonides makes a related point in support of constant personal
   reflection:

   > One who sins a single sin has inclined himself and the entire world toward
   > guilt and causes its destruction; one who performs a single good deed has
   > inclined himself and the entire world toward merit and causes its deliv-
   > erance and salvation. (Maimonides, *Mishneh Torah*, Hilchot Teshuva 3:4
   > [translated from the original Hebrew])

33. The same is true of military actions that entail some possible loss of innocent
   civilian life. A rule of proportionality, rather than an absolute prohibition, gov-
   erns the rule of law.

34. In a seminar I have co-taught at the Harvard Law School, called Justice and
   Morality in the Plays of Shakespeare, I illustrate to my students that the dif-

ficulty of striking this balance is an important theme of Shakespeare's *Measure for Measure*. See Kenji Yoshino, *A Thousand Times More Fair* (New York: Harper-Collins, 2011), 59–88.

35. The Talmud states,

> A Sanhedrin [ancient Jewish supreme court] that executes one person in seven years is called "murderous." Rabbi Eleazar ben Azariah says [this extends to] once in seventy years. Rabbi Tarfon and Rabbi Akiva say, "Had we been among the Sanhedrin, no one would ever have been executed." Rabbi Simon ben Gamliel responds, "They too would have increased the bloodshed in Israel [that is, by completely removing deterrence]." (Babylonian Talmud, Makkot 7a [translated from the original Hebrew])

An amicus brief submitted by Jewish groups in the 1999 U.S. Supreme Court case *Bryan v. Moore*—which presented the question of whether Florida's use of the electric chair for capital punishment was "cruel and unusual" under the Eighth Amendment—quoted the words of the former Israel Supreme Court justice Menachem Elon (*State of Israel v. Tamir*, 37[iii] P.D. 201 [1983]):

> Jewish Law was particularly insistent on the preservation of even a criminal's rights and dignity during the course of punishment. Maimonides, after dealing with the types of punishment a court may impose, including imprisonment, concludes: "All these matters apply to the extent that the judge deems appropriate and necessary for the needs of the time. In all matters, he shall act for the sake of Heaven and not regard human dignity lightly. . . . He must be careful not to destroy their dignity." According to Jewish law, a death sentence must be carried out with the minimum of suffering and without offense to human dignity. This is based on the biblical verse, "Love your fellow as yourself," and the rule is, "Choose for him a humane death." From this we declare that even a condemned felon is your "fellow."

But see the rabbinic exception for "the needs of the time." The Talmud reports that when an obviously guilty murderer was freed because of the absence of a second witness or warning, he would be confined and fed a mixture of water and barley that caused his death. Babylonian Talmud, Sanhedrin 81b.

36. This mantra, known as "Blackstone's formulation," or "Blackstone's ratio," was expressed by Sir William Blackstone in his eighteenth-century treatise titled *Commentaries on the Laws of England*. Maimonides foreshadows Blackstone's formulation when he writes, "To acquit a thousand guilty persons is preferable to killing one innocent." Maimonides, *Sefer Hamitzvot*, Lo Ta'aseh 290 (translated from the original Hebrew). But see Daniel Epps, "The Consequences of Error in Criminal Justice," *Harvard Law Review* 128 (2015).

37. The critical importance of arriving at an appropriate ratio is best illustrated by the following anecdote: "The story is told of a Chinese law professor, who was listening to a British lawyer explain that Britons were so enlightened, they believed it was better that ninety-nine guilty men go free than that one innocent man be executed. The Chinese professor thought for a second and asked, 'Better

for whom?'" Alexander Volokh, "N Guilty Men," *University of Pennsylvania Law Review* 146 (1997): 211. The punch line of this anecdote is similar to Rabbi Simon ben Gamliel's view, cited in ch. 2, n. 35, *supra*.

38. See Dershowitz, *Genesis of Justice*, 87–88.

39. Steve Mills, "What Killed Illinois' Death Penalty," *Chicago Tribune*, March 10, 2011, http://articles.chicagotribune.com/2011-03-10/news/ct-met-illinois-death-penalty -history20110309_1_death-penalty-death-row-death-sentences; "Anthony Porter: False Testimony by a Purported Eyewitness Landed Anthony Porter on Death Row," Bluhm Legal Clinic, Center on Wrongful Convictions, Northwestern Law.

40. Exodus 32:7–35.

41. I thank Rabbi William Hamilton, who pointed out this irony to me.

42. Exodus 32:32. The original language "mecheini na" is translated by the standard Christian translations as "*please* erase me" or "blot me out, *I pray thee*." Indeed, the word *na* does typically mean "please" (see ch. 3, n. 37, *infra*). But the authoritative first-century translator Onkelos translates this phrase into the Aramaic "mecheini che'an" (erase me *now*). Such a translation removes even a modicum of deferential respect. Indeed, the popular Jewish English translation of Artscroll (Mesorah Publications) does not shy away from the translation "erase me now." There is a fascinating midrash on this verse:

> God said, "When I conquer, I lose. When I am conquered, I gain. I conquered the generation of the flood. But did I not lose, for I destroyed my world? So, too, with the generation of the Tower of Babel. So, too, with the men of Sodom. But at the sin of the golden calf I was conquered; Moses prevailed over me [to forgive their sin], and I gained, in that I did not destroy Israel."

Midrash, Pesikta Rabbati 32b–33a (translation taken from World Scripture, *Argument with God*, http://www.unification.net/ws/theme109.htm).

43. See Nachmanides and Rashbam on Exodus 32:32.

44. A fascinating midrash explicitly depicts Moses as God's teacher. The midrash relays that Moses challenged the passage of the Ten Commandments in which God proclaims that He "remembers the sins of fathers for children and grandchildren," arguing that such a system of vicarious punishment is immoral. God then responded to Moses, "You have taught me! By your life, I will strike out my words and establish yours." According to the midrash, God then proceeded to amend his original statement by adding the following verse in Deuteronomy (24:16): "Parents shall not be put to death for [sins of their] children, and children shall not be put to death for [sins of their] fathers." Bamidbar Rabbah 19. I thank Rabbi William Hamilton for providing this source.

### 3. Abraham Refuses to Argue with God and with His Wife over the Lives of His Children—Failing God's Next Test

1. The Akedah is quite significant in Christianity, as it is interpreted to foreshadow God's sacrifice of his son, Jesus. Klauck et al., *Encyclopedia of the Bible and Its Reception*, 181. (Indeed, in the background of Marc Chagall's *Sacrifice of Isaac*—featured

on the cover of my book *The Genesis of Justice*—one can spot Jesus dragging his cross. I once got a great bargain on another Chagall painting. It was for sale at an auction, but it similarly depicts Jesus on the cross in the background of a painting of a red cow. Few buyers were interested in a Jewish-themed painting with a crucifixion in the background.) The Christian commentary on this passage focuses on Abraham's "obedience amidst unclarity." Christian commentators have reasoned, "God's oath, on the one hand, and Abraham's belief and obedience, on the other, are the pillars of the future of Israel." See Klauck et al., *Encyclopedia of the Bible and Its Reception*, 155.

Muslim commentators similarly believe "that Abraham's willingness and that of his son to undergo the sacrifice brought blessings on them and their descendants." Jane Dammen McAuliffe, *Encyclopedia of the Quran, Volume I A-D* (2001), 10. In Islam, however, the identity of Abraham's son that God commanded him to sacrifice is a matter of great controversy. Levenson, *Inheriting Abraham*, 105. Some Muslim commentators, specifically those who came later, believe that Abraham was commanded to sacrifice Ishmael, his firstborn son from Hagar. McAuliffe, *Encyclopedia of the Quran, Volume I A-D*, 6.

2. My research assistant, Elliot Schwab, surveyed more than sixty of the classic rabbinic sources—including ancient midrashim (such as Midrash Rabbah, Midrash Tanchuma, and Yalkut Shimoni), medieval *rishonim* (such as Rashi, Nachmanides, Ibn Ezra, Rashbam, Rabbeinu Bechaye, and Sforno), post-sixteenth-century *acharonim* (such as *Keli Yakar, Siftei Chachamim, Ohr HaChaim, Meshech Chochma,* the Vilna Gaon, *Kedushat Levi, Sfat Emet,* Maharil Diskin, *Beit Halevi,* Netziv, and Rabbi Samson Raphael Hirsch), and twentieth-century traditional rabbinical commentators (such as *Emet L'yaakov, Drash Moshe, Ma'ayan Beit Hashoevea, Limudei Nisan, MeAvirah DeArah, Ohr Gedalyahu,* and the Brisker Rav)—and he found none that directly relate the Sodom incident to the Akedah.

3. This inconsistency is even more pronounced when viewed from the perspective of medieval commentators who contend that God only *requested*—and did not *command*—that Abraham sacrifice Isaac (see ch. 3, n. 37, *infra*). Yet none of those commentators raise this question.

4. Kierkegaard, in his *Fear and Trembling*, briefly notes this paradox, but he provides no explanation to resolve it. Regarding the Akedah, he writes, "But Abraham had faith. He did not beg for himself in hope of moving the Lord; it was only that time when the just punishment had been proclaimed upon Sodom and Gomorrah that Abraham came forward with his prayers." Søren Kierkegaard, *Fear and Trembling*, trans. Alastair Hannay (Harmondsworth, U.K.: Penguin Books, 1985), 54.

5. Several modern commentators do seek to reconcile the two Abrahams. One commentator has claimed that Abraham decided to argue with God over the sinners of Sodom because he had no personal stake in the outcome, since he knew that God would save his nephew Lot, even if He destroyed the rest of the city along with its sinners. He could be certain, therefore, that his argument for justice was pure and uninfluenced by personal considerations. See Rabbi Eliyahu E. Dessler,

*Strive for Truth*, trans. Aryeh Carmell (Nanuet, N.Y.: Feldheim, 1999), 5:96–97. According to this interpretation, one might distinguish the two stories, because the Akedah involved Abraham's beloved son, about whose fate he could not be objective. Accordingly, he could not be certain that an argument he might offer in the name of justice would be pure and uninfluenced by his personal interest in the outcome. The Nobel laureate Elie Wiesel suggests such a reconciliation in his book *Messengers of God* (New York: Random House, 1976), 92–94.

Lippman Bodoff, a contemporary writer, asks, "So how do we begin to explain, or conceive of, an Abraham at the *Akedah* rushing off, without doubt or question, to obey a Divine command to sacrifice Isaac?" In his excellent book *The Binding of Isaac, Religious Murders, and Kabbalah* (New York: Devora, 2005), he seeks to answer this question. Ibid., 28. His basic answer is the following: Instead of challenging God this time, Abraham decided to pursue a "nobler course." His objective was to leave it to God to "pronounce for all, and for all time, the prohibition against murder," thereby demonstrating to the world that God's moral law against murder exists in the absence of a human plea for compassion. Ibid., 48. The problem with this answer is that God does not, in the Akedah story, "pronounce for all, and for all time, the prohibition against murder," or child sacrifice. God never tells Abraham or the world that it would have been wrong for Abraham to sacrifice his son. To the contrary, God's angel appears to praise Abraham for his willingness to do just that: "For now I know that you are a God-fearing man, since you have not withheld your son, your only son, from me." Had God condemned Abraham for his apparent willingness to sacrifice his son, perhaps generations of Jews who sacrificed their children rather than having them convert, or pretend to convert as some did at the time of the Inquisition, would not have chosen that path. See *supra*, pp. 47–51.

6. For a modern midrash on this verse, Rabbi William Hamilton has suggested to me that the phrase "I did not laugh" perhaps means "I will not bear Isaac." In the original Hebrew, the root of the term for laugh—*tzachak*—is the same as the root of Isaac's name (Yitzchak).

7. Sir Walter Scott, *Marmion: A Tale of Flodden Field* (Boston: Ginn, 1891), 244 (canto 6, sec. 17, line 532).

8. Indeed, this is the interpretation that the classical rabbinic commentators seem to take for granted. See Nachmanides, Sforno, and *Ohr HaChaim* on this verse. Genesis Rabbah (48:20), however, takes "He" to mean God. (This divergence is interesting, as it is rare for the classic medieval rabbinic commentators completely to ignore the simple translation of the Midrash.) The standard Christian English translations are divided on whether to spell "he" with a capital *H* or not.

9. To be sure, Sarah is included in midrashic accounts. According to one midrash, after God ordered Abraham to sacrifice Isaac, Abraham went into his tent, and "he spoke these words to [Sarah]: 'My son Isaac is grown up, and he has not yet studied the service of God. Now, tomorrow I will go and bring him to Shem and Eber his son, and there will learn the way of the Lord.'" Louis Ginzberg, *Legends of the Jews*, trans. Henrietta Szold and Paul Radin (Philadelphia: Jewish Publica-

tion Society, 2003), 1:225–26. Similarly, according to one Islamic version of this story—where the Bible's Hagar and Ishmael are substituted for Sarah and Isaac, respectively—Abraham lied to Hagar, instructing her to "wash Ismail and put his best clothes on, for today I want to take him to see my best friend." Knappert, *Islamic Legends*, 1:78.

10. Two verses after this one, the Bible records, "The angel of God called to Abraham a second time from heaven. And he said, 'By myself I swear—the word of God—that because you have done this thing, and have not withheld your son, your only one, that I shall surely bless you.'" One midrash reads into this unsolicited assurance that Abraham had pleaded with God, "Swear to me that you will not test me or my son Isaac anymore." Quoted in Miller, *Abraham*, 181. This would be yet another example of Abraham's requesting a binding covenant from God.

11. Several commentators, however, point to God's earlier promise as a factor that made the test even more troubling to Abraham. Rashi says that Abraham was praiseworthy for not doubting God's ways in the face of this paradox. Rashi, Numbers 6:1. In fact, according to one early manuscript of a medieval midrash, Abraham later boldly informed God, "Had I retorted to You, You would have had no counter[-]retort to me!" See Spiegel, *Last Trial*, 91. According to another midrash, Abraham indeed questioned God—only later. This midrash relays that when the angel of God swooped down at the last moment and told Abraham not to sacrifice his son, Abraham finally protested,

> Yesterday You said ". . . since through Isaac will offspring be considered yours"; You subsequently retreated and said "Please take your son . . ."; and now You say to me "Do not stretch out your hand against the lad?!" (Genesis Rabbah 56:12 [translated from the original Hebrew])

(The midrash concludes that God responded that He had asked Abraham merely to *take* his son and *bring him up* the mountain with the intention of sacrificing him, a commandment that Abraham indeed fulfilled.)

Many commentators raise the obvious question: Why did Abraham wait until this moment to challenge God in this way? Several of the traditional commentators answer that while Abraham was disturbed by this question from the start, he kept it to himself, fearing that he was driven by personal bias. Only later, once God's perplexing sequence of commands called for a leniency that Abraham's personal bias would have swayed him gladly to accept, he felt justified in posing the question. See, for example, Siftei Chachamim, Genesis 22:12; compare with Dessler, *Strive for Truth*, ch. 3, n. 5 *supra*.

12. While the text does not tell us whether Abraham was apprised of the details of Ishmael's miraculous rescue, Abraham was indeed aware of the fact that Ishmael survived, at least according to the traditional rabbinic commentaries. On the verse at the beginning of the Akedah, which states that Abraham "took his two young men with him," the commentaries identify the two as Ishmael and Eliezer. See, for example, Rashi, Genesis 22:3, quoting Leviticus Rabbah 26:7. (Inciden-

tally, while some English versions of the Bible translate the Hebrew *ne'arav* in this verse as "servants," the phrase "young men"—used by the King James Bible, Artscroll, and others—is a more accurate translation.)

13. Abraham's no-brainer predicament seems to be the direct inverse of Thomas Moore's tongue-in-cheek logic, expressed in his poem "An Argument":

> I've oft been told by learned friars
> That wishing and the crime are one,
> And Heaven punishes desires
> As much as if the deed were done.
> If wishing damns us, you and I
> Are damned to all our heart's content;
> Come, then, at least we may enjoy
> Some pleasure for our punishment!

14. This theory is supported by Abraham's words to his servants "I and the lad . . . will return to you," suggesting that Abraham planned all along to return with Isaac intact. One midrash—which apparently refuses to accept that Abraham intended to go all the way—explains this statement as a prophecy that both Abraham and Isaac would return peacefully. Midrash Tanchuma, Vayeira 23. Later medieval commentators clarify, however, that the statement must have been what we would call a Freudian slip: this would not have been much of a "test" had Abraham known the ending all along. See *Eitz Yoseph*, Midrash Tanchuma, Vayeira 23 (citing *Yifei Tohar*). See also Rashi, Genesis 22:5.

15. See Spiegel, *Last Trial*, 82–120.

16. See Levenson, *Inheriting Abraham*, 81–82. Surprisingly, Levenson doesn't expressly raise the conflict between the faithless and the faithful Abraham.

17. Immanuel Kant, *The Conflict of the Faculties*, trans. Mary J. Gregor (New York: Abaris Books, 1979), 115. But see Levenson, *Inheriting Abraham*, 107–8:

> The effect of Kant's thinking is to remove the Aqedah from the realm of narrative and theology and to relocate it foursquare within the domain of ethics. Once the story is analyzed as an ethical parable, Abraham, of course, can be only a negative model. How could it ever be ethical to kill an innocent boy in cold blood?

18. Woody Allen, *Without Feathers*, in *The Complete Prose of Woody Allen* (New York: Wings Books, 1991), 36.

19. Bob Dylan, *Highway 61 Revisited* (Columbia Records, 1965).

20. Kierkegaard, *Fear and Trembling*, 44.

21. See Babylonian Talmud, Baba Metzia 59b. This question about who has the authority to interpret the text of a governing document has recurred throughout history. A recent example was Chief Justice Roberts's interpretation of the Affordable Care Act's penalty clause as a tax on those who don't buy insurance, although Obama and drafters of the bill had insisted previously that the mandate was not a tax.

22. The Rabbi Eliezer story was written, of course, by rabbis, who had a stake in promoting rabbinic authority to interpret the Torah, just as the justices who wrote the opinion in *Marbury v. Madison* had a stake in promoting judicial authority to interpret the Constitution. In his celebrated treatise on halachic prophecy, Rabbi Philip Fishel Schreiber shows that according to Maimonides and others, prophecies prior to the giving of the Torah were ineffectual on the prophet's audiences, but they were indissolubly binding on the prophet himself. See Rabbi Philip Fishel Schreiber, "*HaEmunah BeNevuah UNevuas Moshe Rabbeinu*," in *Likkutei Aveidah* (Jerusalem: Mossad Harav Kook, 2012), 329–30.

23. Kierkegaard, *Fear and Trembling*, 103.

24. Ibid., 85.

25. See Jonathan Sacks, *Future Tense* (London: Hodder & Stoughton, 2009), 193–95, in which Chief Rabbi Sacks insists that God's statement "Shall I conceal from Abraham that which I do?" constituted a direct invitation to Abraham to become "part of the judicial process"—a "juror" to God's "judge."

26. Aside from suspending his rational instincts, Abraham had to suspend his natural compassion for his son. According to one version of an ancient midrash, Abraham told God afterward, "I suppressed my feelings of pity in order to do thy will." Spiegel, *Last Trial*, 90.

27. Kierkegaard, *Fear and Trembling*, 85; see also ibid., 88.

28. Luke 14:26. It is difficult, on its face, to reconcile this purported statement from Jesus with the commandment to honor and obey one's father and mother, especially because Jesus said he was not changing the laws of the Torah. Many interpretations of this challenging verse have been offered. See Arthur A. Just Jr., ed., *Luke*, Ancient Christian Commentary on Scripture, New Testament III (Downers Grove, Ill.: InterVarsity Press, 2003), 240–41.

29. There is a Hasidic concept of making oneself a fool in worship of God, which was possibly influenced by this verse in Corinthians. See, for example, Jerome Gellman, *Abraham, Abraham: Kierkegaard and the Hasidim on the Binding of Isaac* (Burlington, Vt.: Ashgate, 2003), 17, citing Rabbi Nachman of Breslov. It is also possible, of course, that the Christian concept was influenced by early Jewish theological interpretations of the Akedah and other biblical accounts of Jewish fundamentalism.

30. Spiegel, *Last Trial*, 90.

31. Rabbi Moshe Weissman, *The Midrash Says* (Brooklyn: Benei Yakov, 1980), 1:205. The quotation here is a rough translation of the words of the fourteenth-century Talmudist Nissim ben Reuven (also known by his acronym, the Ran). *Derashot HaRan HaShalem* (Hebrew) (Jerusalem: Mossad Harav Kook, 2003), 239–40.

32. Kierkegaard, *Fear and Trembling*, 53–54.

33. The circumstances surrounding More's martyrdom are familiar, especially to those who have seen the stage play or the film *A Man for All Seasons*. When the pope refused to accept King Henry's marriage to Anne Boleyn, Henry created the Church of England, which the king was to head. Parliament enacted a mandatory oath, which required More and other officials to swear allegiance to this new arrangement.

Thomas More, who was the lord high chancellor and a devoted Catholic, refused to either sign the oath or explain his refusal. In standing up to the king and Parliament, More followed in the tradition of both Abraham the faith-driven zealot and Abraham the clever lawyer.

It was More the religious zealot who refused to sign the oath. It was More the lawyer who refused to explain his refusal, arguing that in the absence of an explanation—a confession—he could not be convicted of high treason, because the prosecutor could not prove what everyone inferred from his silence.

Notwithstanding this and other arguments, More was convicted and sentenced to die. He then explained that he had no choice but to refuse, because he was commanded to sign by secular law but commanded not to sign by religious law. When the king commands one action and God commands another, a religious zealot has no choice. This is the way More reportedly put it: "The Act of Parliament is like a sword with two edges, for if a man answer one way, it will confound his soul, and if he answer the other way, it will confound his body."

More followed God's order and gave up his life on earth for the promise of eternal salvation in the hereafter—a promise God did not make to Abraham with regard to Isaac. For his heroic martyrdom, More has been accorded the honor of sainthood.

I have never quite understood why religious zealots, who firmly believe they will be rewarded in the hereafter by doing God's will and dying, are regarded as heroes. For them, the choice is a tactical one that serves their own best interest. It is a simple consequence of a religious cost-benefit analysis. Thomas More seemed to understand this far better than those who have lionized him over the centuries.

To a religious zealot who believes that the soul is forever and the body merely temporary, it is a simple matter to choose the edge of the sword, which will cut off his life but preserve his soul. Heaven and hell are forever, while life on earth—especially for a man of More's age—is only a matter of a few years. So, if More was a true believer in reward and punishment after life, he was no hero. He was merely a religious zealot who, by choosing death over damnation, demonstrated nothing more than his abiding belief in reward and punishment after life and made a wise trade-off by which he gave up a few years on earth for an eternity in heaven. That should earn him a place of honor in the pantheon of true believers but not in the pantheon of heroism.

Only if More had been, in fact, a hypocrite—a man who feigned belief in the hereafter but who was really a secret nonbeliever—would he deserve the status of hero, but then he would be denied the accolade of true belief, as well as of honesty.

There is, to be sure, an intermediate position. More could have been someone who tried hard to believe but could not suppress his doubts. If that was the case, then his decision to choose death entailed some degree of risk. Maybe he was giving up a bird in his earthly hand, namely what was left of his life, for two in the heavenly bush, namely his chance at heaven. But this, too, would be a calculation, albeit a more complex and probabilistic one. Indeed, the familiar argument for religious observance—one that was given to me as a youth—is simply a variation on this cost-benefit theme. If there is no God, then you lose nothing but a few hours of wasted prayer by erroneously acting as if there were one, but if there is a God—who rewards and punishes in accordance with your devotion to Him—then you lose a great deal by erroneously acting as if there were none. There is thus a significant tactical advantage in being religious. But that simple formula—called Pascal's wager, after the seventeenth-century French philosopher and mathematician who articulated it—only works when the choice does not require the person choosing to give up anything as important as his life, or the life of his son. It is easy to pray occasionally in order to maximize your odds of reward in the hereafter, even if you seriously doubt there is anyone to listen to your prayers. But if you are asked to bet an earthly life on heaven and hell, then the stakes increase dramatically.

But they are stakes nonetheless, and in More's situation he had to make the bet. Indeed, he tried not to, by refusing to answer the questions: "Wherefore, I will make thereunto no other answer because I will not be occasion to the shortening of my life." No dice! You've got to choose, replied the king's prosecutor. At this point, a calculating but doubting cost-benefit maximizer would have to decide whether to place his existential currency on his earthly or his heavenly life. Other factors—such as the physical pain associated with death, how history would judge him, or how his family might be treated here on earth if he chose the calculated risk of heaven—could well figure into the calculation. But at bottom, he would have to resolve his doubts and make a calculated and wise choice.

I am not suggesting that religious zealots actually think that way consciously, but surely these factors enter into the mix of belief, calculation, and action at some level. Although there is no textual proof that Abraham made a similar calculation, some commentators suggest that he might have.

The basic question still remains: Why is it more noble for a firm believer to do something because God commanded it than because the king commanded it—if the believer believes that God is more powerful than a king? In general, submission to the will of a powerful person has not been regarded as especially praiseworthy—except, of course, by the powerful person. Would Thomas More have joined the genocidal Crusades or the notorious Inquisition just because God and the pope commanded them? Would he have sacrificed his children if God or the pope had asked him to? If so, would he justly be regarded as a hero? Nor is this question applicable only to Christian believers. Should Jews praise Abraham for his willingness to kill his own son just because God commanded it? Would Abraham have been willing to engage in genocidal behavior—as some biblical figures did—just because God commanded it? A true hero—even one who believed in a God who rewards and punishes—would have resisted that unjust command and risked God's wrath, just as a true hero would have refused God's order to murder heathen women and children during the Crusades. And just as heroic soldiers throughout history have resisted the command of their superiors to commit war crimes. We hear little about such heroic resisters to God's alleged immoral commands, because these heroes are generally killed and relegated to the dustbin of history.

34. I'm reminded of the joke about God's showing a young sinner the punishments of hell. The sinner sees Hitler making love to Marilyn Monroe and exclaims, "This is how you punish Hitler?" to which God responds, "You don't understand. He's her punishment!"

35. E. E. Reynolds, *The Trial of St. Thomas More*, special ed. (New York: Notable Trials Library, 1993), 153.

36. From what we do know from the trial, it appears that the real Thomas More was campaigning hard for sainthood from the outset of the case. He made repeated comparisons between himself and other saints:

> More have I not to say, my Lords, but that like the Blessed Apostle St. Paul as we read in the Acts of the Apostle, was present and consented to the death of Saint Stephen, and kept their clothes that stoned him to death, and yet be they now both twain Holy Saints in heaven, and shall continue there friends together for ever, so I verify trust, and shall therefore right heartily pray, that though your lordships have now here in earth been judges to my condemnation, we may hereafter in heaven merrily all meet together, to our everlasting salvation. And thus I desire Almighty God to preserve and defend the King's Majesty and to send him good counsel. . . . But if I should speak of those that are already dead, of whom many be now Holy Saints in heaven, I am very sure it is the far greater part of them that, all the while they lived, thought in this case that way that I think now, and therefore am I not bounden, my Lord, to conform my conscience to the Council of one Realm against the General Council of Christendom. (Ibid., 131–32, 124)

37. Quoted in Nehama Leibowitz, *Studies in Bereshit (Genesis)*, trans. Aryeh Newman, 4th ed. (Jerusalem: Hemed Press, 1981), 189. According to the fourteenth-century Talmudist Nissim ben Reuven (Ran), God only requested—but never commanded—that Abraham sacrifice Isaac. See *Derashot HaRan HaShalem*, 238–39. Like other medieval rabbinic commentators—such as Rashi and Nachmanides—he derives this interpretation from God's words "kach na et bincha" (literally, "*please* take your son"). See Rashi and Ramban on Genesis 22:2. The Ran ventures a step further than they do, however, by claiming that Abraham would not have received any punishment had he disobeyed God's "request." The Ran goes on to explain that God could not possibly have made such a command, which contradicted his earlier promise to continue the covenant through Isaac's progeny. Instead, God "requested" that Abraham waive this promise. See *Deroshat HaRan HaShalem*, 238–39.

38. In a 1787 letter to his seventeen-year-old nephew Peter Carr, Jefferson wrote, "Question with boldness even the existence of a God; because, if there be one, he must more approve of the homage of reason, than that of blindfolded fear." Jefferson to Carr, Aug. 10, 1787, in *The Life and Selected Writings of Thomas Jefferson*, ed. Adrienne Koch and William Peden (New York: Franklin Library, 1982), 350; see also Alan Dershowitz, *Blasphemy: How the Religious Right Is Hijacking Our Declaration of Independence* (Hoboken, N.J.: John Wiley & Sons, 2007), 16–18.

39. Isadore Twersky, *A Maimonides Reader* (New York: Behrman House, 1972), 83. This quotation from Maimonides alludes to the words of Antigonus of Socho, who said, "Do not be like servants who serve their masters for the sake of reward; rather, be like servants who do not serve their masters for the sake of reward." Mishnah, Avot 1:3. In fact, some medieval commentators cite an alternative text of the Mishnah, which reads, "Rather, be like servants who serve their masters *for the sake of not receiving reward*." See Rabbeinu Yonah to Mishnah, Avot 1:3 (italics added). Similarly, in Jewish thought, "repentance out of love" is considered a higher spiritual attainment than "repentance out of fear." Babylonian Talmud, Sotah 31a.

40. The modern commentator Yehuda Jacobowitz similarly contrasts Abraham's many acts of compassion with his seemingly cold separation from his nephew Lot after tensions arose between their shepherds (Genesis 13:7–9). According to Jacobowitz, Abraham set aside his inclusionary tendencies in an effort to illustrate to his nephew the importance of distancing oneself from harmful influences. Jacobowitz, *MeAvirah DeArah*, 5–7.

41. See *Pninim Me'Shulchan HaGRA* (Jerusalem: Moreshet Hayeshivot, 1997), 46–47; cf. Ecclesiastes 3:1–8 ("Everything has its season . . ."). This interpretation of the Vilna Gaon is reminiscent of an ancient Greco-Roman parable (with Socrates or Aristotle as the hero), which was reincarnated as a Hasidic tale about Moses roughly during the Gaon's lifetime:

> When Moses became famous for leading the Israelites out of Egypt, an Arabian king sent an artist to the Israelite camp with orders to capture and bring to the king, a portrait of Moses. Upon receipt of the portrait, the king convened his physiognomists and charged them with the preparation of a character analysis of Moses, so that the king would know wherein lay the strength of Moses. The report was not a pleasant one. Moses was described as capricious, greedy, arrogant, indeed as being evil to the core. The king rebuked his physiognomists for their patently absurd analysis. . . . The king decided to resolve the matter by a state visit to the Israelite camp in the Wilderness of Sinai. Upon sighting Moses, the king knew at once that the artist's depiction was perfect. The king concluded that his physiognomists were incompetent. However, during a chat with Moses, Moses explained that by inclination he was all that the physiognomists had described, even worse. Only sustained self-discipline and sheer determination enabled him to overcome his natural inclination, and to attain the stature and glory that were now his. (See Shnayer Z. Leiman, "R. Israel Lipschutz: The Portrait of Moses," *Tradition* 24, no. 4 [Summer 1989]: 91–98)

Spiegel (*Last Trial*, 90–91) cites four differing early midrashic versions of a legend according to which Abraham prayed to God that his suppression of his instinct to challenge God serve as a merit for his descendants when they are in distress. There is a prayer included in standard Jewish prayer books—likely based on this legend—that beseeches God to allow his mercy to overpower his anger, in the way that Abraham's boldness overpowered his compassion during the Akedah.

42. The Talmud posits that Abraham's *yirah* (fear) of God mentioned in this context was "out of love." The Talmud there goes on to say that one who serves God out of love is greater than one who serves Him out of *yirah* (fear). Babylonian Talmud, Sotah 31a. It is difficult to make sense of this Talmudic passage. Whatever the intended meaning of *yirah* is, how can the Talmud distinguish *yirah* from *ahava* (love)—by saying the latter is greater than the former—and then claim that the *yirah* mentioned regarding Abraham was "out of love"? Perhaps the Talmud's intention is that a fear that stems from love is greater than a basic fear of punishment.

43. For example, Ibn Ezra summarily dismisses the version whereby Isaac was killed and subsequently revived as being "contrary to the text." Ibn Ezra, Genesis 22:19. But see Spiegel, *Last Trial*, addressing several obscure midrashic accounts that have Abraham actually killing Isaac.

44. The Bible records only that Abraham "stretched out his arm and took the knife," after which the angel warns, "Do not stretch out your hand against the lad," implying that Abraham had not yet done so.

45. The Midrash posits that Abraham had tears in his eyes but that his "heart" was joyous to fulfill his Creator's will. Genesis Rabbah 56:11. This conflicting evidence would have to be weighed by a jury.

46. According to one midrash, Isaac asked that his father bind him, in order to prevent his body from squirming out of uncontrollable fear. Ibid.

47. The Talmud, apparently taking for granted that Isaac knowingly and willingly went along with Abraham's original plan, addresses the question of how Isaac could even have believed the Akedah prophecy that his father presumably relayed to him. See Babylonian Talmud, Sanhedrin 89b, and Rashi there. The treatise on halachic prophecy by the brilliant scholar Rabbi Philip Fishel Schreiber includes a discussion on whether—and under what framework—Isaac would have been required to obey such an aberrant prophecy. Schreiber, "*Ha-Emunah BeNevuah UNevuas Moshe Rabbeinu*," 328–37.

48. The text suggests that no actual physical (as distinguished from psychological) harm came to Isaac, but some rabbinic commentators refer to "the blood of the Binding of Isaac." See Levenson, *Inheriting Abraham*, 94, quoting Mechilta d'Rabbi Ishmael.

49. Midrash Hagadol, Vayeira 19.

50. Genesis Rabbah 56:11.

51. Ibid.

52. Midrash Hagadol, Vayeira 19.

53. According to one midrash, Sarah died from shock when she heard about her son's brush with death. See Rashi, Genesis 23:2, citing Midrash Tanchuma. But the question arises, who told Sarah? According to the Tannaic Midrash Pirkei d'Rabbi Eliezer, it was the evil angel Samael. Quoted in Miller, *Abraham*, 187.

54. Interestingly, the Bible provides no account of their speaking to each other before the Akedah either. They spoke only *during* this traumatic event. The sixteenth-century rabbinic commentary *Keli Yakar* posits that Isaac opens that conversation by saying merely "Father!" but nothing else, because he had already sensed Abraham's tragic plan, and the son thus concluded that Abraham had morphed

into a cruel dominator who no longer possessed fatherly love for him. He therefore calls him "Father" to see if Abraham had totally relinquished his fatherly role. Then, when Abraham lovingly responds, "Yes, my son," Isaac doubts his earlier conviction and asks, "Here are the firestone and the wood; but where is the sheep for the burnt offering?" Abraham responds, "God will see to the sheep for His burnt offering, my son," hinting that this was God's Will and not a scheme he devised on his own. Only then, "the two of them walked on together," as opposed to before this discussion, when there was a disconnect between the two. *Keli Yakar*, Genesis 22:7. However, according to Avot of Rabbi Natan (700–900 C.E.), "Isaac went along with Abraham with his mouth but in his heart he was saying, 'Who will save me from my father? I have no help other than God.' " Avot of Rabbi Natan, quoted in Miller, *Abraham*, 168.

55. Isaac blesses his two sons—who themselves fight bitterly over the "primary" blessing—and Jacob pronounces individual blessings and parting words for each of his twelve sons, as well as for two of his grandsons. Genesis 27, 48–49.

56. He gave gifts to his other children by a different mother, "while he was still living," but waited until he was dead to will the rest to Isaac.

57. It is also noteworthy that God never speaks to Abraham after the Akedah, implying perhaps that God was disappointed with Abraham's willingness to sacrifice his son.

58. See my discussion regarding Abraham's burial of Sarah, pp. 53–5, *supra*.

59. Joseph Story, "The Value and Importance of Legal Studies," in *The Miscellaneous Writings of Joseph Story*, ed. William W. Story (Boston: C. C. Little and J. Brown, 1852), 523.

60. Rabbi Levi Yitzchak Berditchev, the eighteenth-century Hasidic master, filed such a lawsuit against God in a religious court (*beit din*). See Anson Laytner, *Arguing with God* (Northvale, N.J.: Aronson, 1990), 179–96.

61. David Hartman, *A Living Covenant* (Woodstock, Vt.: Jewish Lights, 2012), 44–45. The references to David and Donniel Hartman were provided by Rabbi Lauren Berkun of the Shalom Hartman Institute.

62. Spiegel, *Last Trial*, 15.

63. Ibid., 22.

64. It is remarkable to me that the words "Crusades" and "crusaders" today convey positive connotations. I once wrote to the then president of the College of the Holy Cross in Worcester, Massachusetts, urging him to consider changing the name of its athletic teams from the Crusaders, to which he responded in an angry letter, telling me, in effect, to mind my own business. It would have been good if the Crusades, which were motivated by Christian animus against Muslims, had not been the business of Jews. But on the way to battle Muslims in Jerusalem, the crusaders murdered thousands of Jewish babies, women, and men only because they were Jewish.

65. Spiegel, *Last Trial*, 25–27. But see one of the sorrowful poems written during that era:

O Lord, Mighty One dwelling on high!
Once, over the Akedah, Ariels cried out before Thee.

But now how many are butchered and burned!
Why over the blood of children did they not raise a cry? . . .
Now one Akedah follows another, they cannot be counted.
(Ibid., 20–21)

66. Wiesel, *Messengers of God*, 71.
67. Ibid., 90.
68. Ibid., 95–96.
69. See Genesis 21:6.
70. Wiesel, *Messengers of God*, 97.
71. See William Styron, *Sophie's Choice* (New York: Random House, 1979), and Alan Dershowitz, *Chutzpah* (New York: Touchstone, 1992), 179.
72. A few years ago, a radical Israeli yeshiva published a book called *Torat Hamelech* (The king's Torah), which argued that the biblical prohibition against murder applies only "to a Jew who kills a Jew" and called non-Jews "uncompassionate by nature." Presented as a "halachic" (Jewish law) compendium, the book posited that one may kill children of Israel's enemies, because "it is clear that they will grow to harm us." Daniel Estrin, "Rabbinic Text or Call to Terror?," *Jewish Daily Forward*, Jan. 20, 2010. The bigoted book was condemned by the leading Israeli rabbis, and those responsible were arrested and prosecuted for inciting violence. See Elad Benari, "Rabbi Ovadia Yosef Opposes 'Torat Hamelech' Book," *Arutz Sheva*, June 30, 2011, http://www.israelnationalnews.com/News/News.aspx/145306 #.U2kufK1dV6o.
73. Deuteronomy 2:26–29, as quoted in Donniel Hartman, "Judaism: Between Religion and Morality," in *Judaism and the Challenges of Modern Life*, ed. Moshe Halbertal and Donniel Hartman (New York: Continuum, 2007), 50.
74. Hartman, "Judaism," 55.
75. Ibid., 57.
76. Ralph Waldo Emerson, *The Essay on Self-Reliance* (Aurora, N.Y.: Roycrofters, 1908), 23.

## 4. Abraham Negotiates to Buy a Burial Cave for Sarah

1. But see Nachmanides's commentary on this verse, in which he refuses to accept that the two were separated. He suggests instead that Abraham happened to be away on a trip when Sarah died.
2. In Judaism, shiva is the weeklong mourning period for immediate family members of a deceased.
3. The Talmud notes that Ephron first offered the field as a gift, but when push came to shove, he quoted Abraham the exorbitant sum of four hundred shekels. Babylonian Talmud, Baba Metzia 87a. The Talmud posits that this illustrates the rabbinical theme that whereas righteous people say little and do much, evil people promise much but do little. Ibid. This principle echoes Shammai's mantra, "Say little and do much." Mishnah, Avot 1:15.
4. Chrysostom, an early Church Father, praises Abraham's character and sense of justice in his insistence on paying for the plot of land: "Notice, however, how

the good man instructs even those people with his characteristic common sense, through his very actions, by forbearing to take possession of it before paying a just price." Drawing on Abraham's actions, Chrysostom advised, "Woe to those who pile house on house and add property to property for the purpose of robbing their neighbor of something. . . . This good man . . . did not behave in that fashion; instead, he insisted on buying the tomb, and, when he saw those from whom he sought it ready and willing to hand it over, he could not bring himself to accept it before he paid the right price." Sheridan, *Genesis 12–50*, 118.

5. See Alan Dershowitz, *Taking the Stand* (New York: Crown, 2013), 474n16.

## Part II.   In the Footsteps of Abraham:
## Jews on Trial, as Defendants and Defenders

### Introduction

1. A revisionist history of Herzl argues that although Herzl himself claimed, "What made me a Zionist was the Dreyfus trial," the issue was far more complex and the roots of his Zionism were deeper in his upbringing and his psyche. See Georges Yitzhak Weisz, *Theodor Herzl: A New Reading* (Jerusalem: Gefen, 2013), 30, 29–43.

2. See Alan Mittleman, Jonathan D. Sarna, and Robert Licht, eds., *Jewish Polity and American Civil Society* (Lanham, Md.: Rowman & Littlefield, 2002), 30.

3. I have been called "Israel's single most visible defender—the Jewish state's lead attorney in the court of public opinion." "Forward 50 2007," *Jewish Daily Forward*, http://forward.com/forward-50-2007/.

4. See pp. 133–6, *supra*, for a more detailed discussion of who is a Jewish lawyer.

5. *Krulewitch v. United States*, 336 U.S. 440, 458 (1949) (Jackson dissenting).

### 5.  The Trial of Jesus, the Conviction of the Jews, and the Blood Libel

1. Dershowitz, *Taking the Stand*, 377.

2. This claim lives on in some circles until this day. Recently, the Center for Near East Policy Research discovered a textbook published by the Palestinian Authority and distributed to 492,000 students which teaches that "the Jews" murdered Jesus in the "Palestinian city of Jerusalem." Center for Near East Policy Research to author, e-mail, April 2, 2014.

3. Quoted in Barbara Dancygier, *Viewpoint in Language: A Multimodal Perspective* (Cambridge, U.K.: Cambridge University Press, 2012), 25.

4. See Mendel Beilis, *Blood Libel: The Life and Memory of Mendel Beilis* (CreateSpace, 2011).

5. "Israeli Couple Saved from Mob in Kiev," *Virtual Jerusalem*, March 16, 2014, http://www.virtualjerusalem.com/news.php?Itemid=12366.

6. Geoffrey Chaucer, *The Prioress's Tale* (Norman: University of Oklahoma Press, 1987), 17. See also, E. M. Rose, *The Murder of William of Norwich*, Oxford, 2015.

7. Joseph Jacobs, *Jewish Ideals, and Other Essays* (New York: Macmillan, 1896), 203–4.

8. Judith R. Baskin, ed., *The Cambridge Dictionary of Judaism and Jewish Culture* (Cambridge, U.K.: Cambridge University Press, 2011), 520.

9. Walter Laqueur, *The Changing Face of Antisemitism: From Ancient Times to the Present Day* (Oxford: Oxford University Press, 2006), 56.

10. Martin Gibson, "No Choice but to Speak Out—Israeli Musician 'a Proud Self-Hating Jew,' " *Gisborne Herald*, Jan. 23, 2009, http://philum.info/24915.

11. See Alan Dershowitz, "Why Are John Mearsheimer and Richard Falk Endorsing a Blatantly Anti-Semitic Book?," *New Republic*, Nov. 4, 2011, http://www.newrepublic.com/article/politics/97030/atzmon-wandering-who-anti-semitism-israel.

12. Gilad Atzmon, *The Wandering Who? A Study of Jewish Identity Politics* (Winchester, U.K.: Zero Books, 2011), 185.

13. Gilad Atzmon, "Truth in Stuttgart, Israel Worse Than Nazi Germany," *Veterans Today*, Feb. 19, 2011, http://www.veteranstoday.com/2011/02/19/truth-in-stuttgart/.

14. See *Obsession: Radical Islam's War Against the West*, dir. Wayne Kopping (Clarin Project, 2007).

15. A contemporary Christian variation of this libel was pushed by the Honduran cardinal Óscar Andrés Rodríguez Maradiaga, who was on the short list for pope. He has claimed that "the Jews" are to blame for the scandal surrounding the sexual misconduct of priests toward young parishioners! According to his conspiracy theory, "the Jews" wanted to get even with the Catholic Church for its anti-Israel positions while at the same time deflecting attention away from Israeli injustices against the Palestinians. He then went on to compare the "Jewish controlled" media to "Hitler." See John L. Allen Jr., "A Whiff of Anti-Semitism in Rome's Assessment of Sex Abuse Crisis; a Boost for Tettamanzi; Lawyers Target Holy See," *National Catholic Reporter*, July 19, 2002, http://www.nationalcatholicreporter.org/word/pfw0719.htm. See also Alan Dershowitz, "Virulent Anti-Semite on Short List to Become Next Pope," *National Post*, Feb. 22, 2013, http://fullcomment.nationalpost.com/2013/02/22/alan-dershowitz-virulent-anti-semite-on-short-list-to-become-next-pope/.

16. Michael Fruend, "Passover, Blood Libels, Then and Now," *Jerusalem Post*, April 13, 2014, http://www.jpost.com/Jewish-World/Judaism/Passover-blood-libels-then-and-now-348382.

17. Ibid. The article was finally removed after receiving criticism.

18. See Michael Burns, *Dreyfus: A Family Affair* (New York: HarperCollins, 1991).

## 6. Alfred Dreyfus, Leo Frank, Rudolf Slansky, Anatoly Sharansky, and the Nation-State of the Jewish People on Trial

1. For more thorough treatments of the Dreyfus trial discussed in this chapter, see Jean-Denis Bredin, *The Affair: The Case of Alfred Dreyfus* (Birmingham, Ala.: Notable Trials Library, 1989), and Burns, *Dreyfus*.

2. See Genesis 39.

3. See Alan Dershowitz, *America on Trial: Inside the Legal Battles That Transformed Our Nation* (New York: Warner Books, 2004).

4. The full text of the letter is translated in Émile Zola, *The Dreyfus Affair: "J'Accuse" and Other Writings*, trans. Eleanor Levieux (New Haven, Conn.: Yale University Press, 1998), 43–52.

5. Bredin, *Affair*, 351–52.

6. Ibid., 352.

7. See Theodor Herzl, *The Jewish State* (n.p.: Filiquarian, 2006).

8. For a more thorough treatment of the Leo Frank trial discussed in this chapter, see Leonard Dinnerstein, *The Leo Frank Case* (Birmingham, Ala.: Notable Trials Library, 1991).

9. Ibid., 149–50.

10. See Mittleman, Sarna, and Licht, *Jewish Polity and American Civil Society*, 30.

11. Dinnerstein, *Leo Frank Case*, 166–67. Although the actual ballad was composed by "Fiddlin'" John Carson only after the trial, its sentiments were expressed loudly and clearly during the trial and subsequent legal proceedings.

12. See *Frank v. Mangum*, 237 U.S. 309, 349–50 (1915) (Holmes dissenting):

> The single question in our minds is whether a petition alleging that the trial took place in the midst of a mob savagely and manifestly intent on a single result is shown on its face unwarranted, by the specifications, which may be presumed to set forth the strongest indications of the fact at the petitioner's command. This is not a matter for polite presumptions; we must look facts in the face. Any judge who has sat with juries knows that, in spite of forms, they are extremely likely to be impregnated by the environing atmosphere. . . .
>
> [S]upposing the alleged facts to be true, we are of opinion that if they were before the supreme court, it sanctioned a situation upon which the courts of the United States should act; and if, for any reason, they were not before the supreme court, it is our duty to act upon them now, and to declare lynch law as little valid when practised by a regularly drawn jury as when administered by one elected by a mob intent on death.

13. See Matthew Mark Silver, *Louis Marshall and the Rise of Jewish Ethnicity in America: A Biography* (Syracuse, N.Y.: Syracuse University Press, 2013), 161.

14. Steve Oney, *And the Dead Shall Rise* (New York: Pantheon, 2003), 589.

15. There is a fascinating and largely unknown ethical story behind the public legal story of the Frank case. It turns out that while Leo Frank was on death row, one of Atlanta's most prominent lawyers, Arthur Gray Powell, learned that Frank was innocent and that another man—presumably the government's star witness—was the killer. Powell described the case in his memoir:

> Subsequent to the trial, and after his conviction had been affirmed by the Supreme Court, I learned who killed Mary Phagan, but the information came to me in such a way that, though I wish I could do so, I can never

reveal it as long as certain persons are alive. We lawyers, when we are admitted to the bar, take an oath never to reveal the communications made to us by our clients. (Arthur Gray Powell, *I Can go Home Again* [University of North Carolina Press, 1943], p. 291)

The eminent lawyer was forced into the most excruciating legal, ethical, and moral dilemma a professional can possibly confront. The ethical rules of the profession were clear. There was no available exception to the rule mandating confidentiality of privileged communications about past crimes. That still left the moral and personal issue of whether any human being—regardless of his or her profession—can and should allow a preventable miscarriage of justice to be carried out, especially in a capital case.

In a typically lawyerlike way, the eminent lawyer in the real case apparently saw to it that the governor learned the information known to him, but without his own "fingerprints" being on the communication. This is how he put it: "Without ever having discussed with Governor Slaton the facts which were revealed to me, I have reason to believe, from a thing contained in the statement he made in connection with the grant of the commutation, that, in some way, these facts came to him and influenced his action." (Powell, ibid.) But the eminent lawyer's compromise did not work. Although the governor did commute Leo Frank's sentence, he was not able to persuade a vengeful public of Frank's innocence. I doubt that Frank would have been lynched had the eminent lawyer come forward and disclosed his information. Instead, his client almost certainly would have been lynched.

16. See "Statement of Alonzo Mann" in Dinnerstein, *Leo Frank Case.*
17. See "Pardon," Georgia State Board of Pardons and Paroles, March 11, 1986. An image of the original document is available at www.gpb.org/files/georgiastories/nsouthfrank176.jpg.
18. For a more thorough treatment of the Slansky trial discussed in this chapter, see Meir Cotic, *The Prague Trial: The First Anti-Zionist Show Trial in the Communist Bloc* (New York: Cornwall Books, 1987).
19. As another example of Abrahamesque name change, Slansky was born with the more Jewish-sounding middle name Salzmann. His full name was Rudolf Salzmann Slansky. He dropped the Salzmann.
20. "Tragicomedy in Prague," *New York Times*, Nov. 22, 1952, 22.
21. During the Great Purge of the 1930s, Stalin—who publicly condemned anti-Semitism but practiced it throughout his life—imprisoned and often killed writers, intellectuals, artists, and politicians whom he viewed as a threat to his program of Communism. He specifically targeted Jews, including prominent politicians such as Lev Kamenev, Leon Trotsky, and Grigory Zinoviev. In 1939, Stalin ordered Molotov to "purge" completely the Ministry of Foreign Affairs of Jews. Echoes of this program continued throughout the subsequent decades. In 1948, a popular Jewish actor-director named Solomon Mikhoels was killed in a suspicious car accident. On August 12, 1952, the "Night of the Murdered Poets," Joseph Stalin had thirteen of the most celebrated Yiddish writers, poets, actors,

and other intellectuals executed. In the 1960s, aliya activists were charged with "disseminating anti-Soviet propaganda." In 1970, eleven people were charged with trying to hijack a plane to escape the Soviet Union en route to Israel. Similar "trials," some of which resulted in death sentences, continued throughout the 1970s. See Robert Conquest, *The Great Terror: Stalin's Purge of the Thirties* (London: Macmillan, 1973); Cotic, *Prague Trial*, 235–55; and Joshua Rubenstein and Vladimir P. Naumov, eds., *Stalin's Secret Pogrom* (New Haven, Conn.: Yale University Press, 2001). See also Telford Taylor, *Courts of Terror* (New York: Random House, 2012).

22. See Louis Rapoport, *Stalin's War Against the Jews: The Doctors' Plot and the Soviet Solution* (Toronto: Free Press, 1990).

23. See Alan Dershowitz, "Some Hard Questions About the Western European Double Standard Against Israel," *Jerusalem Post*, March 12, 2014, http://www.jpost.com/Opinion/Op-Ed-Contributors/Some-hard-questions-about-the-Western-European-double-standard-against-Israel-345171.

24. Natan Sharansky, *Fear No Evil* (New York: PublicAffairs, 1998), 222.

25. Individual leaders of Israel have been threatened with prosection in the International Criminal Court. "Court to Look into Possible Israeli War Crimes in Palestinian Territories," *New York Times*, Jan. 16, 2015.

26. Quoted in Silvan Shalom, "A Fence Built for Peace," *Guardian*, Feb. 2, 2004, http://www.theguardian.com/world/2004/feb/03/comment. Other Jewish leaders objected to the resolution by proclaiming that Jews should, and generally do, deplore all forms of racism. As Shimon Schwab, a leading New York rabbi, declared in response to the resolution, "We are Jews who hate Racism because we all have been the foremost victims of Racism. We hate racism because all men were created in G-d's image." Reprinted in Rabbi Shimon Schwab, *Selected Writings* (Lakewood, N.J.: CIS, 1988), 148.

27. Video footage of Moynihan's speech is available at http://www.youtube.com/watch?v=Z_8VqP7QKPA.

28. UN General Assembly Resolution 46/86 (1991).

29. Irwin Cotler, *Voices on Anti-Semitism* (podcast), June 5, 2008, available at http://www.ushmm.org/confront-antisemitism/antisemitism-podcast/irwin-cotler.

30. Ibid.

31. Ibid.

32. Tom Lantos, "The Durban Debacle: An Insider's View of the UN World Conference Against Racism," *Fletcher Forum of World Affairs* 26, no. 1 (Winter/Spring 2002): 31, 37.

33. Video footage of my Durban speech is available at http://www.youtube.com/watch?v=DDOA3_vZIzc.

34. See BDS Movement, http://www.bdsmovement.net/. See also Jennifer Medina, "Student Coalition at Stanford Confronts Allegations of Anti-Semitism," *New York Times*, April 15, 2015, p. A11.

35. In defending Israel, I have offered the following ten reasons that BDS, not Israel, should be placed on trial and convicted:

1. The BDS movement immorally imposes the entire blame for the continuing Israeli occupation and settlement policy on the Israelis. It refuses to acknowledge the historical reality that on at least three occasions, Israel offered to end the occupation and on all three occasions, the Palestinian leadership, supported by its people, refused to accept these offers.

2. The current BDS movement, especially in Europe and on some American university campuses, emboldens the Palestinians to reject compromise solutions to the conflict.

3. The BDS movement is immoral because its leaders will never be satisfied with the kind of two-state solution that is acceptable to Israel. Many of its leaders do not believe in the concept of Israel as the nation-state of the Jewish people. (The major leader of the BDS movement, Marwan Barghouti, has repeatedly expressed his opposition to Israel's right to exist as the nation-state of the Jewish people, even within the 1967 borders.) At bottom, therefore, the leadership of the BDS movement is opposed not only to Israel's occupation and settlement policy but to its very existence.

4. The BDS movement is immoral because it violates the core principle of human rights: namely, "the worst first." Israel is among the freest and most democratic nations in the world. It is certainly the freest and most democratic nation in the Middle East. When a sanction is directed against only a state with one of the best records of human rights, and that nation happens to be the state of the Jewish people, the suspicion of bigotry must be considered.

5. The BDS movement is immoral because it would hurt the wrong people: it would hurt Palestinian workers who will lose their jobs if economic sanctions are directed against firms that employ them. It would hurt artists and academics, many of whom are the strongest voices for peace and for an end to the occupation. It would hurt those suffering from illnesses all around the world who would be helped by Israeli medicine and the collaboration between Israeli scientists and other scientists.

6. The BDS movement is immoral because it would encourage Iran—the world's leading facilitator of international terrorism—to unleash its surrogates, such as Hezbollah and Hamas, against Israel, in the expectation that if Israel were to respond to rocket attacks, the pressure for BDS against Israel would increase, as it did when Israel responded to thousands of rockets from Gaza in 2008–2009.

7. The BDS movement is immoral because it focuses the world's attention away from far greater injustices, including genocide.

8. The BDS movement is immoral because it promotes false views regarding the nation-state of the Jewish people, exaggerates its flaws and thereby promotes a new variation on the world's oldest prejudice, namely anti-Semitism. It is not surprising therefore that the BDS movement is featured on neo-Nazi, Holocaust denial and other overtly anti-Semitic websites and is promoted by some of the world's most notorious haters such as David Duke.

9. The BDS movement is immoral because it reflects and encourages a double

standard of judgment and response regarding human rights violations. By demanding more of Israel, the nation-state of the Jewish people, it expects *less* of other states, people, cultures, and religions, thereby reifying a form of colonial racism and reverse bigotry that hurts the victims of human rights violations inflicted by others.

10. The BDS movement will never achieve its goals. Neither the Israeli government nor the Israeli people will ever capitulate to the extortionate means implicit in BDS. They will not and should not make important decisions regarding national security and the safety of their citizens on the basis of immoral threats. Moreover, were Israel to compromise its security in the face of such threats, the result would be more wars, more death, and more suffering. Alan Dershowitz, "Ten Reasons Why BDS Is Immoral and Hinders Peace," Haaretz, Feb. 12, 2014, http://www.haaretz.com/opinion/.permium-I .573880.

36. See Alan Dershowitz, *Terror Tunnels: The Case for Israel's Just War Against Hamas* (New York: RosettaBooks, 2014).

37. Quoting this poem in a letter, the Supreme Court justice Oliver Wendell Holmes once remarked, "To me it is queer to see the wide-spread prejudice against the Jews. I never think of the nationality and might even get thick with a man before noticing that he was a Hebrew." Quoted in Brad Snyder, "The House That Built Holmes," *Law & History Review* 30, no. 3 (2012): 721n333.

38. Burke blamed the French Revolution on "Jew brokers," despite the absence of any Jews in its leadership. See Michael Walzer, "Imaginary Jews," *New York Review of Books*, March 20, 2014.

39. See ibid.

40. Ibid.

41. Daniel Schwammenthal, "The Israel-Bashing Club," *Wall Street Journal*, Sept. 3, 2007, http://online.wsj.com/news/articles/SB118877270728215947.

42. See Alan Dershowitz, *The Case Against Israel's Enemies* (Wiley, 2008) pp. 8-9.

43. Quoted in "The Covenant of the Hamas—Main Points," Federation of American Scientists, Article 22, https://www.fas.org/irp/world/para/docs/880818a.htm.

44. See, for example, Rense.com, RePortersNoteBook.com, TheOccidentalObserver .net, *Jhate*.

45. The Anti-Israel British member of Parliament George Galloway accused "the Zionists" of orchestrating the recent conflict in Ukraine in order to bring "these Nazis to power in Kiev," thereby forcing Ukrainian Jews "to go and settle in Palestine." Elad Benari, "Galloway Claims Israel Engineered the Unrest in Ukraine," *Arutz Sheva*, April 3, 2014, http://www.israelnationalnews.com/News /News.aspx/179217#.UoKHZq1dV6o.

46. See Julian Kossoff, "Missing Malaysia Airlines MH370: The Jews Are to Blame, Surely?," *International Business Times*, March 12, 2014, U.K. edition, http://www .ibtimes.co.uk/missing-malaysia-airlines-mh370-jews-are-blame-surely-1440019. As it turned out, the apparent free pass was too good to be true. Several days after the above-cited article was published, the usual anti-Jewish and anti-Israel con-

spiracy theorists began to crawl out of the woodwork, even blaming the Jewish-controlled media for this so-called silence. See, for example, Jeff Rense and Yoichi Shimatsu, "Flt 370 . . . Israeli Double-Cross," YouTube, https://www.youtube .com/watch?v=OBZlkMQiTZQ; "Malaysian Flight MH370: Is THIS What Happened to the 'Missing' Plane?," *Northerntruthseeker*, March 26, 2014, http:// northerntruthseeker.blogspot.com/2014/03/malaysian-flight-mh370-is-this-what .html ("The Jewish controlled media was busy misleading everyone into the false belief that the plane crashed somewhere off the coast of Sumatra, Indonesia in the eastern Indian Ocean"); "Flight 370 Clone in Storage at Tel Aviv Airport," *Before It's News*, March 26, 2014, http://beforeitsnews.com/alternative/2014/03 /flight-370-clone-in-storage-at-tel-aviv-airport-2926768.html.

### 7. The Jewish Lawyer as Abrahamic Idol Smasher, Advocate, Collaborator, Rescuer, and Deal Maker

1. William Shakespeare, *Henry VI, Part II*, act 4, scene 2.
2. Indeed, some of the leading nineteenth-century Orthodox rabbis embraced Darwinism as a God-guided phenomenon. See, for example, Rabbi Israel Lipschutz, *Tiferet Yisrael, Drush Ohr HaChaim* (printed in the back of *Mishnayot Yachin uBoaz*, Sanhedrin), 3; Rabbi Samson Raphael Hirsch, *Collected Writings of Rabbi Samson Raphael Hirsch* (New York: Feldheim, 1984), 7:263–64; Rabbi Naftali Zvi Yehuda Berlin, *Ha'amek Davar*, on Genesis 7:23; Rabbi Eliyahu Benamozegh, *Em L'Mikra* (Leghorn and Paris, 1862–65), on Deuteronomy 22:10. But see Rabbi Meir Leibush Wisser, Malbim on Genesis 7:20, positing that burning waters from the Flood caused accelerated fossilization; Moshe Feinstein, *Igrot Moshe* (New York: Noble Press, 1982), 6:323 (Yoreh De'ah 3:73), ruling that evolutionary theory is tantamount to heresy.
3. Legally educated radicals who can be included under "idol smashers" include Thomas More, Thomas Jefferson, John Adams, John Jay, Giuseppe Mazzini, Maximilien Robespierre, Jacques-Pierre Brissot, Judah Benjamin, Charles de Calonne, Karl Marx, Vladimir Lenin, Moisei Uritsky, Rosa Luxemburg, Christian Rakovsky, Nikolai Krylenko, Chen Jiongming, Mahatma Gandhi, Eleftherios Venizelos, Theodor Herzl, David Ben-Gurion, Ze'ev Jabotinsky, Yitzhak Shamir, Menachem Begin, Meir Kahane, Jan Karski, Abraham Lincoln, Jawaharlal Nehru, Jacques Vergès, Fidel Castro, Nelson Mandela, Bob Hepple, James Kantor, Harold Wolpe, Arthur Chaskalson, Stanley Levison, William Kunstler, and Lynne Stewart. Some studied law but never practiced.
4. Jonathan Kaufman, *A Hole in the Heart of the World* (New York: Penguin, 1997), 42.
5. Sanford Levinson, "Identifying the Jewish Lawyer," *Cardozo Law Review* 14 (1993).
6. For a discussion of whether there are uniquely Jewish ways of practicing law, see *supra*, pp. 133–6.
7. Tibor Krausz, "The Enemy Within," The Jerusalem Report, *Jerusalem Post*, March 24, 2014, 7–8, http://www.jpost.com/Jerusalem-Report/Israel/The -enemy-within-344254.

8. Roy Isacowitz, "Mandela's Jewish Comrades," *Haaretz*, July 30, 2013.

9. See Hugh Adler, "The Jews in Mussolini's Italy," *Holocaust and Genocide Studies* 23, no. 2 (Fall 2009).

10. See *The Best Defense* (New York: Random House, 1982); *Chutzpah*; *Taking the Stand*; *Courts of Terror* (New York: Knopf, 1976).

11. See Dershowitz, *Best Defense*, chap. 1.

12. The debates can be seen on YouTube.

13. Matthew 5:17.

14. Jerold S. Auerbach, *Unequal Justice: Lawyers and Social Change in Modern America* (New York: Oxford University Press, 1976), 71.

15. Ibid.

16. Ibid.

17. "Mene, Mene, Tekel Upharsin," *Wall Street Journal*, Feb. 1, 1916, 1. The article alludes to the "attorney for the people" but never calls Brandeis by name, instead referring to him snidely as "this man." The title of the article is a reference to Daniel 5:25, in which the Jewish prophet Daniel spots a disembodied hand writing those cryptic words on the wall and correctly interprets it as an omen that the king would be killed that night.

18. While it might come as a surprise that Lowell would turn his back on one of the university's most esteemed alumni, one must keep in mind that this was the same Harvard president who had implemented admissions policies designed to limit sharply the number of Jewish students in the institution. See Dershowitz, *Chutzpah*, 67–68.

19. "Contend Brandeis Unfit: Dr. Lowell and 54 Bostonians Submit Petition to Senate," *New York Times*, Feb. 13, 1916, 16.

20. Ibid.

21. Bruce Afran et al., eds., *Jews on Trial* (Jersey City: Ktav, 2005), 157–58.

22. Ibid., 157.

23. Ibid., 154.

24. Ibid., 160.

25. See Douglas G. Morris, *Justice Imperiled* (Ann Arbor: University of Michigan Press, 2005), 1:

    The judiciary's right-wing bias was documented from the outset. A young statistician, Emil Julius Gumbel, began to chronicle it in 1921 and 1922 in two publications, with the chilling, but apt, titles *Zwei Jahre Mord* (Two Years of Murder) and *Vier Jahre politischer Mord* (Four Years of Political Murder). He compiled the political crimes committed by rightists and leftists between late 1918 and the summer of 1922 and the number of resulting prosecutions, convictions, and sentences. The right wing had committed 354 murders, which resulted in no death sentences, one life sentence, a total of 90 years and 2 months in prison, and 326 unpunished perpetrators; the left wing had committed 22 murders, which resulted in ten death sentences, three life sentences, a total of 248 years and 9 months in prison, and 4 unpunished perpetrators.

26. Ibid., 3.
27. Ibid.
28. See ibid., 132–55.
29. Ibid., 297.
30. Ibid., 302–3.
31. The Anti-Defamation League advocates rights for all, but as a Jewish organization it prioritizes Jewish rights.
32. Mishnah, Avot 1:14.
33. See René Cassin, "How the Charter on Human Rights Was Born," *UNESCO Courier*, Jan. 1968.
34. Ibid., 6.
35. This tragic phenomenon is the reverse of Isaiah 2:4, in which the prophet describes a utopian time of world peace, when militants "shall beat their swords into plowshares, and their spears into pruninghooks."
36. For an account of Ginsburg's life, see her Biography.com entry, http://www .biography.com/people/ruth-bader-ginsburg-9312041, and her *Judgepedia* entry, http://judgepedia.org/index.php/Ruth_Bader_Ginsburg. Regrettably, I could not locate any full-length, adult-level biographies on her. I look forward to what are sure to be fascinating forthcoming biographies on her colorful career. A video recording of her inspiring 2013 interview with Dean Martha Minow at Harvard Law School can be seen on YouTube. "A Conversation with Ruth Bader Ginsburg at HLS," YouTube, http://www.youtube.com/watch?v=umvkXhtbbpk.
37. See Judges 4. Another reference to the Old Testament is on display in Justice Ginsburg's chambers, in the form of a banner bearing the words "Justice, justice thou shalt pursue." "A Conversation with Ruth Bader Ginsburg at HLS."
38. She has quipped that had she secured a job at a law firm, she would be just another retired law firm partner today. "A Conversation with Ruth Bader Ginsburg at HLS."
39. William J. Clinton, "Remarks Announcing the Nomination of Ruth Bader Ginsburg to Be a Supreme Court Associate Justice," June 14, 1993, American Presidency Project, http://www.presidency.ucsb.edu/ws/?pid=46684.
40. While Karski was not Jewish, he married a Polish Jewish dancer named Pola Nirenska in 1965. See E. Thomas Wood and Stanislaw M. Jankowski, *Karski: How One Man Tried to Stop the Holocaust* (New York: John Wiley & Sons, 1994), 275.
41. See Jan Karski, *Story of a Secret State* (London: Penguin, 2011), and Wood and Jankowski, *Karski*.
42. Karski, *Story of a Secret State*, 347–67.
43. Ibid., 378–80.
44. It is interesting to note in this context an uncharacteristically personal dissenting opinion Frankfurter penned, in which he distanced himself from his Jewish identity vis-à-vis his professional duties. A landmark 1943 Supreme Court case presented the question of whether a group of Jehovah's Witnesses could be forced to comply with a state law compelling schoolchildren and teachers to salute the American flag. The group's religious doctrine considered a flag a "graven image,"

which should not be saluted (see Exodus 20:4). Frankfurter, a Viennese immigrant to America, opined,

> One who belongs to the most vilified and persecuted minority in history is not likely to be insensible to the freedoms guaranteed by our Constitution. Were my purely personal attitude relevant I should whole-heartedly associate myself with the general libertarian views in the Court's opinion, representing as they do the thought and action of a lifetime. But as judges we are neither Jew nor Gentile, neither Catholic nor agnostic. We owe equal attachment to the Constitution and are equally bound by our judicial obligations whether we derive our citizenship from the earliest or the latest immigrants to these shores. As a member of this Court I am not justified in writing my private notions of policy into the Constitution, no matter how deeply I may cherish them or how mischievous I may deem their disregard. The duty of a judge . . . is not that of the ordinary person. It can never be emphasized too much that one's own opinion about the wisdom or evil of a law should be excluded altogether when one is doing one's duty on the bench. (*West Virginia State Board of Education v. Barnette*, 319 U.S. 624, 646–47 [1943]).

45. David S. Wyman, *The Abandonment of the Jews* (New York: Pantheon, 1984), 316.
46. Jerold S. Auerbach, *Rabbis and Lawyers* (Bloomington: Indiana University Press, 1990), 163–65.
47. To be sure, the analogy is imperfect. Frankfurter refused to question *Roosevelt*, who was not the source of the Nazi atrocities, whereas Abraham refused to question God, when God commanded *him* to personally sacrifice Isaac.
48. Richard Breitman and Alan M. Kraut, *American Refugee Policy and European Jewry, 1933–1945* (Bloomington: Indiana University Press, 1987), 74.
49. Senator Theodore Bilbo, a proud Ku Klux Klan member, would refer to Jews as "kikes" during Senate proceedings. Robert L. Fleegler, "Theodore G. Bilbo and the Decline of Public Racism, 1938–1947," *Journal of Mississippi History* (Spring 2006): 16, http://mdah.state.ms.us/pubs/bilbo.pdf.

    Sadly, such cultural stereotypes have not totally disappeared, even at the level of government legislatures. As recently as April 2013, the Oklahoma state representative Dennis Johnson casually used the expression "Jew me down on a price" during a legislative debate. After someone passed him a note informing him of his "faux-pas," he added with a smile, "Did I? All right. I apologize to the Jews. They're good small businessmen as well. All right, folks. Let's get back to this."

    The episode is available on a YouTube video, in which fellow members of the Oklahoma state legislature—which does not contain a single Jew—can be seen snickering and then heard openly laughing. "Oklahoma State Rep Dennis Johnson Says 'Jew Down the Price' During Floor Debate," YouTube, http://www.youtube.com/watch?v=uJlws6SWviI; Dan Amira, "Oklahoma Lawmaker Uses the Term 'Jew Me Down' and Everybody Laughs, Because Oklahoma," *New York*, April 18, 2013, http://nymag.com/daily/intelligencer/2013/04/oklahoma-jew-me-down-dennis-johnson-video.html.

Following the murder of three non-Jews by a neo-Nazi who was trying to kill Jews, the mayor of Marionville, Missouri, said he agreed with some of the sentiments expressed by the killer about the "Jew-run government-backed banking industry" and the Jewish-run Federal Reserve and the corporations that "are run by Jews" and that are "destroying us." Mary Moloney, "Marionville Mayor: I Agree with Frazier Miller's Beliefs, Not Behaviors," KSPR (ABC) 33, April 15, 2014, http://www.kspr.com/news/local/marionville-mayor-i-agree -with-frazier-millers-beliefs-not-behaviors/21051620_25503568.

50. John Shelton Lawrence and Robert Jewett, *The Myth of the American Superhero* (Grand Rapids, Mich.: Eerdmans, 2002), 132.

51. An online version of Ford's entire book series called *The International Jew* is available—compliments of the American Nazi Party—at http://americannazi party.com/about/InternationalJew.pdf.

52. After visiting Germany in 1936, Lindbergh speculated that "Hitler must have far more character and vision than I thought existed in the German leader, who has been painted in so many different ways by the accounts in America and England." The historical record indicates that Lindbergh's sympathies for Hitler extended to the latter's views toward Jews. Henry Ford once quipped, "When Charles [Lindbergh] comes out here, we only talk about Jews." Max Wallace, *The American Axis: Henry Ford, Charles Lindbergh, and the Rise of the Third Reich* (New York: St. Martin's Press, 2003), 155, 289.

53. Directed by Elia Kazan (1947), who was not Jewish.

54. See Haskel Lookstein, *Were We Our Brothers' Keepers? The Public Response of American Jews to the Holocaust, 1938–1944* (New York: Vintage, 1988).

55. For a thorough treatment of Judah Benjamin's colorful career, see Eli N. Evans, *Judah P. Benjamin: The Jewish Confederate* (New York: Free Press, 1988).

56. See ibid., 15–22. In a classic illustration of the rabbinic mantra "ma'aseh avot siman libanim" (loosely translated: "the actions of parents are repeated by their children"), Benjamin's father was himself expelled from the very synagogue that he founded. Ibid., 207.

57. Yulee converted to Christianity after marrying the daughter of the governor of Kentucky and eventually denied his Jewish heritage, claiming instead that he descended from a Moroccan prince! Ibid., 48.

58. Carl Sandburg, *Abraham Lincoln: The Prairie Years and the War Years* (New York: Harcourt, Brace & World, 1954), 239.

59. Judah P. Benjamin, *A Treatise on the Law of Sale of Personal Property* (London: H. Sweet, 1868).

60. Evans, *Judah P. Benjamin*, 56.

61. See Robert N. Rosen, *The Jewish Confederates* (Columbia: University of South Carolina Press, 2000).

62. Southern Clergyman, *A Defence of Southern Slavery Against the Attacks of Henry Clay and Alexander Campbell* (Hamburg, S.C.: Robinson & Carlisle, 1851), 5. I own this pamphlet, having found it in a flea market in Miami Beach.

63. Ibid.

64. Since Kreisky's death, Greece and Hungary might well have overtaken Austria for this dishonor.

65. Robert S. Wistrich, *Anti-Zionism and Anti-Semitism: The Case of Bruno Kreisky* (Hebrew University, 2007), 20.
66. Ibid., 26.
67. See Dershowitz, *Taking the Stand*, 276–78, 428–31.
68. See "19 Kislev: The 'New Year' for Chassidim," Chabad, http://www.chabad.org/library/article_cdo/aid/335659/jewish/19-Kislev-The-New-Year-of-Chassidism.htm.
69. "Statement by Irwin Cotler on Russian Travel Ban," March 24, 2014, http://irwincotler.liberal.ca/blog/statement-irwin-cotler-russian-travel-ban/.
70. Alan Dershowitz to the Norwegian Nobel Committee, Jan. 23, 2008.
71. See Linda Atkinson, *In Kindling Flame: The Story of Hannah Senesh, 1921–1944* (New York: Beech Tree Books, 1992).
72. Malcolm Gladwell, *Outliers: The Story of Success* (New York: Back Bay Books, 2011), 122–23.
73. Ibid., 116–20.
74. Ibid., 119.
75. Ibid., 120.
76. See Levinson, "Identifying the Jewish Lawyer."

## Epilogue: The Future of Abraham's Descendants

1. Deuteronomy 16:20.
2. Leviticus 19:16.
3. A version of this classic Jewish joke was featured in the 1971 film *Fiddler on the Roof.* See "Fiddler on the Roof—Perchik," YouTube, Sept. 13, 2009, http://www.youtube.com/watch?v=qXIdamBEUJE.
4. Auerbach, *Unequal Justice*, 107.
5. Ibid., 127.
6. Ibid., 125.
7. Ibid.
8. The current chairman of Sullivan & Cromwell—historically one of the most elite white-shoe firms—is a Sabbath-observant Orthodox Jew. At the same time, many of the Jewish law firms have become some of the most prestigious firms. One of the most elite firms in New York today is called Wachtell, Lipton, Rosen & Katz!
9. See "Lydia E. Kess," interview with Barbara Bensoussan, "Striking a Balance: Work & Family," *Jewish Action*, Nov. 21, 2012, http://www.ou.org/jewish_action/11/2012/striking-a-balance-work-family/.
10. See Alan Dershowitz, *The Vanishing American Jew: In Search of Jewish Identity for the Next Century* (New York: Touchstone, 1998).
11. For an up-to-date and comprehensive study of Jewish American identity and cultural trends, see the Pew Research 2013 survey of Jewish Americans, http://www.pewresearch.org/topics/jews-and-judaism/.
12. See Greg Smith and Alan Cooperman, "What Happens When Jews Intermarry?,"

Pew Research Center, Nov. 12, 2013, http://www.pewresearch.org/fact-tank/2013/11/12/what-happens-when-jews-intermarry/.

13. Sanford Levinson, "Identifying the Jewish Lawyer," 14 *Cardozo Law Review* 1577 (1993): 1582.

14. See Stephanie Mitchell, "A Look Inside: Eliot House," *Harvard Gazette*, April 19, 2012, http://news.harvard.edu/gazette/story/2012/04/eliot-house/.

15. Leviticus 19:16.

16. Ibid. 19:14.

17. The ancient Aleinu prayer recited at the end of every Jewish service contains the phrase "letakein olam bemalchus shadai"—repair the world under God's sovereignty. The concept of "tikkun olam"—repairing the world—was first expounded upon in Lurianic kabbalah and was later popularized by the Hasidic, Mussar, and Conservative movements.

18. Compassion is one of the thirteen attributes of God that Jews are instructed to emulate. Maimonides, *Mishneh Torah*, Hilchot Deot 1:11.

19. See Deuteronomy 16:20 ("Justice, justice shall thou *pursue*").

20. Babylonian Talmud, Sanhedrin 17(a).

21. Though recently, a Hasidic Jew, who disapproved of a client I was representing, shouted at me, "It was Jews like you that brought about the Holocaust."

22. I also described a non-Jewish judge that way. See "Mensch on the Bench: Alan M. Dershowitz Remembers Harry A. Blackmun as Remarkably Open and Fair-Minded," *Los Angeles Times*, March 5, 1999, B7.

23. For a contrary view, see the landmark U.S. Supreme Court case *Citizens United v. Federal Election Comission, 558 U.S. 310 (2010)*.

24. Perhaps this is true because these values are not uniquely Jewish but have been adopted by many Jews because of our history. See Dershowitz, *Vanishing American Jew*.

25. Milton Himmelfarb, "The Jewish Vote (Again)," *Commentary*, June 1973.

26. In 1996, 74 percent of Jewish voters surveyed in Northern and Southern California voted against Proposition 209—which passed overwhelmingly, ending most forms of affirmative action in California. See *Los Angeles Jewish Times*, Nov. 22, 1996, 9.

27. Babylonian Talmud, Baba Batra 12b.

28. Ecclesiastes 3:1.

# INDEX

# Index

# Index